THE
WOW
BOOK

Ways of Optimizing Well-being

CARLA LABELLA

◆ FriesenPress

One Printers Way
Altona, MB R0G 0B0
Canada

www.friesenpress.com

Copyright © 2024 by Carla LaBella
First Edition — 2024

All rights reserved.

Cover image: Adobe Stock Photo

This publication contains the opinions of its author in regard to the subject matter covered. It is sold with the understanding that neither the author nor the publisher is engaged in rendering medical or health-care advice. While the author has used her best efforts in preparing this book, the reader is encouraged to consult with their medical and/ or health-care professional before adopting any of the suggestions and strategies shared in this book. The author and publisher disclaim any liability for any damage or loss caused, directly or indirectly, by information contained in this book.

ISBN
978-1-03-830443-8 (Hardcover)
978-1-03-830442-1 (Paperback)
978-1-03-830444-5 (eBook)

1. SELF-HELP, PERSONAL GROWTH, HAPPINESS

Distributed to the trade by The Ingram Book Company

TABLE OF CONTENTS

ACKNOWLEDGMENTS

This book would not have been possible without the incredible group of people I have surrounded myself with throughout my life. Each of these persons has impacted my life in big and small ways, from a small gesture of support, sharing words of encouragement, to having my back when I screwed up and needed a nudge (or push!) to move forward. I will be forever grateful for your support, your inspiration, and the opportunity to learn and become better.

Thank you to my real-life Mr. Keating (a reference to Robin Williams in *Dead Poets Society*), Mr. Coons, my high-school law and history teacher. Thank you for inspiring me to become a teacher and to appreciate the written word. Your belief that I could do better forced me to raise the bar, and to reflect more deeply on the topics explored in your classes and beyond. Thank you to Dr. Dick Day for your enthusiasm in the classroom and on those VHS tapes in my first-year psychology classes. You were my first teacher to introduce me to psychology, a discipline I would quickly fall in love with, in my studies and in my career. I am also grateful that you gave me the opportunity to work as an undergraduate teaching assistant, as it reinforced my love for teaching. Thank you to Drs. Daphne Maurer and Terri Lewis at McMaster University's Infant Vision Laboratory for taking a chance on me as a research assistant in your lab. I learned so much from you—especially how to pay attention to the details, a skill that was instrumental in writing and revising this book. To the late Dr. Lee Brooks, my undergraduate thesis advisor at McMaster University, and Dr. Derek Koehler, my graduate thesis advisor at the University of Waterloo: Thank you for helping me hone my critical thinking and research skills. You spent countless hours with me as we developed our research programs. Collectively, the skills and knowledge I learned from each of you allowed me to take on the task of writing this book.

I am grateful to my friend Jacqui Candlish for encouraging me to study positive psychology more than 10 years ago. After contemplating different programs to study for my sabbatical, I decided to pursue a certificate in applied positive psychology with Emiliya Zhivotovskaya and her team at the Flourishing Center in New York City. Although there are many opportunities to learn positive psychology today, back then there wasn't a single program in Canada. I was a sponge, soaking it all in as I was introduced to the science of well-being and happiness. I brought my learning to Mohawk College and created the Positive Psychology Hub, co-facilitated the Happiness Series with Basilia Iatomasi and then Stephanie Hart, and co-developed the Positive

Psychology course with Tulsie Raghubir-Mamouzellos. Over the years, our team has grown exponentially, and I am grateful to be able to collaborate with this inspiring group of like-minded individuals. My learning continued a couple of years ago when I decided to apply for a second sabbatical, this time to study mindfulness and yoga. At the time, I desperately needed to apply in my own life what I had been sharing with others (to go from *knowing* to *doing*). I am grateful for the opportunity to learn mindfulness through Unified Mindfulness, a framework created by Shinzen Young. Thank you to my teachers, Chris DiMeglio and Kelly Baron, other mentors, and my classmates, for taking this journey with me. My experience with this program was life-changing. Thank you also to my many teachers and classmates at Modo Yoga. It was an absolute pleasure to learn about yoga's history, philosophy, and postures (asanas) with you over the course of our time together.

A special thank you to my friends Sid Stacey and Marisa Mariella from the Suicide Prevention Community Council of Hamilton. Over the years, you have allowed me to share these positive psychology lessons with youth, teachers, parents, and community members. Thank you for giving me, and us, a platform to highlight these resilience-building tools and skills.

To my many friends and colleagues at Mohawk College: Thank you for making my time at the college a more enjoyable experience. To my friends in the Department of Liberal Studies: I have learned so much from each of you. Thank you for teaching me things outside of psychology, from history to bones, globalization, sustainability, and social issues. You have all made our conversations at the lunch table and in the hallways a little more interesting. To my sangha group (Kate Dunn, Eugenia Nuta, and Vicky Webb): Our 15 minutes together on weekday mornings to connect and meditate is truly the highlight of my day. Thank you for bringing your warm and generous spirit to our daily sessions.

Thank you to the many students I have had the pleasure to teach over my 20+ years of teaching. I am blessed that I get paid to do what I love. And just as I hope you have learned a thing or two from me over the years, I have learned so much from you. You have been generous with sharing your knowledge with me and asking great questions in class. I love getting questions where I don't know the answer as it forces me to dig in and follow a few rabbit holes before coming to an answer that is usually more complicated than we think! Thank you too for sharing your stories with me; it has been an honour to listen to your inspirational stories of strength and resilience.

To the readers of this book at various stages of the process, my friends

Kate Dunn, Katie George, Basilia Iatomasi, Dr. Joe Kim, Lisa Pender (WOW Tip 11), Sue Popowich, Dan Popowich, Jenn Roberts, and Mary Ann Starcevic: Your thoughtful comments and feedback were very much appreciated and were incorporated into the many revisions of this book. Thank you to my friend Arun Jacob for our countless conversations about the book writing/publishing process, to Lisa Ferguson of Lisa Ferguson Virtual Solutions for your critical eye when editing, typesetting, and designing this book, and to Abby Kompare of Figment Branding for creating the many images and adding the final touches throughout the book. Finally, thank you to FriesenPress, especially Candice Letkeman, for your assistance with proofreading, and to Kayla Lang for the support throughout the production process. I am grateful for your collective efforts in helping me bring this book to life and into the world.

Most importantly, to my family and friends: Since I was young, I have been surrounded by love and support. As a child, you made me believe that I could do and be anything I wanted to be. Thank you for providing me with this loving foundation and a soft space to land if I messed up (which I have, many times). Although I would question my value and worth along the way, it was comforting to know that I had a team of loved ones in my corner. And to my husband, Demetrio, and my boys, Christian and Michael: Demetrio, you have been by my side from the beginning (wow, 30+ years!), and this book would not have been possible without your love and encouragement. Thank you for giving me time on the weekends to write this book, and for taking over tasks around the house so I wouldn't get distracted when writing. Christian and Michael, the two of you are my biggest joys in my life. I am so proud of each of you and what you have accomplished in your lives so far. I can't wait to see what you will put out into the world; I know that it will be a better place with you in it.

What I hope is abundantly clear here is that I could not have written this book without this incredible circle that surrounds me. I am truly blessed by each one of these friendships and relationships. The creation of this book was a team effort. That is the power of *ubuntu* (I am because *we* are). Thank you to all of you.

AS PART OF MY COMMITMENT TO RECONCILIATION

I acknowledge that this book was written on the traditional territory of the Haudenosaunee and Anishnaabeg nations, within the lands protected by the Dish with One Spoon wampum agreement and which is currently home to many Indigenous peoples from across Turtle Island (North America). As a settler, I am grateful for the opportunity to live here, and for the generations of people who have taken care of this land. I recognize and deeply appreciate Indigenous peoples' historic connection to this place and their contributions, both in shaping and strengthening our communities.

Many of the positive psychology concepts and tools that are highlighted in this book have their roots in Indigenous worldviews and ways of being. Over the last few years, it has been my privilege to have been learning from many incredible colleagues at Mohawk College, including Rick McLean, Elizabeth Gray, and Dr. Johanne McCarthy. They have been generous in sharing their wisdom with me. The more I listen and learn, the more I recognize the parallels between my training and learning in psychology and the knowledge that has been passed on for generations among our Indigenous neighbours. As this topic is beyond the scope of this book, I invite you to join me as I commit to continuing to listen to and learn from their beautiful stories and wisdom.

Thank you (Miigwetch),

Carla

INTRODUCTION

Life is a balance between what we can control and what we cannot.
I am learning to live between effort and surrender.

~ Danielle Orner

Men are born soft and supple; dead, they are stiff and hard.
Plants are born tender and pliant; dead, they are brittle and dry.
Thus whoever is stiff and inflexible is a disciple of death.
Whoever is soft and yielding is a disciple of life. The hard
and stiff will be broken. The soft and supple will prevail.

~ Lao Tzu

MY MOTIVATION TO WRITE THIS BOOK

When the pandemic first hit, I had been teaching psychology at the local college for almost 18 years and facilitating self-care/wellness sessions there and in my community. In my Positive Psychology course, my students and I discussed ways we could "flourish" in our personal and professional lives: the importance of sleep, exercise, mindfulness, play, and connection, among other topics. But during March 2020 and for months after, I worked around the clock, 70–80 hours a week, pivoting my courses to an online format. Everything I taught my students was thrown out the window. My five-to-six days per week yoga/barre routine was nonexistent. I woke up every morning and opened my computer, and the last thing I did every night was power it down. I knew the research; I had shared these messages as widely as possible, yet I ignored them when I desperately needed to adhere to these lessons. My body was screaming at me to slow down, to take a break. I was running on fumes, falling back on routines I had grown accustomed to as a young student and worker; just working harder and longer to get it done—and not to the standard of "good enough," but to my usual "as close to perfect" bar that I had strived for since I was young. I was paying a heavy price for this unsustainable way of living and losing patience with the people I loved and cared about most. I was emotional and on edge. Tears streamed down my face in the middle of a yoga class I rarely attended that first pandemic summer. I committed to *do* better moving forward, and to share the wisdom that I had learned over the years in the form of this book. As you will learn, many times the struggle is not with the *knowing* part—because we often know what we *should* be doing when it comes to taking care of ourselves—but the *doing* part. The book's final portion is devoted to going from *knowing* to *doing*.

BASIC THEMES OF THIS BOOK

There are three core and interrelated themes that I will highlight in this book: energy, bendABILITY, and creating space.

Energy

Let's explore this concept of energy, an invaluable resource that fuels our thoughts and actions. Although our physical, cognitive, emotional, and spiritual energy can be replenished and renewed in various ways, it has a finite capacity; we need to exert it wisely and mindfully. Jim Loehr and Tony Schwartz, authors of *The Power of Full Engagement* (2005), coined this concept of *managing energy*.[1] They suggest that by tweaking how we live our lives in terms of how we think, speak, and act, we can expand and renew this energy source to draw on as needed.

With this concept in mind, take a moment to think about where your energy is currently and has been for the last couple of weeks. Are you feeling energetic, depleted, or somewhere in between? Now think about the activities, people, or situations enhancing or depleting your energy. As you work through this book, I hope you make choices for yourself that will increase this renewable energy source. Which energy-enhancing items/activities can you do more of? And likewise, which energy-depleting items/activities can you change, either by eliminating them, minimizing how often you engage in these behaviours, or perhaps setting up much-needed boundaries around these items (or people)? The aim is to be well-resourced as you move through the world. To the best of your ability, you need to make choices: (1) How can you best "fill your energy tank"? and (2) How and do you, in this moment, want to spend this resource? Envisioning a price tag on each choice will help you determine what is worth the underlying energy cost associated with an action. In other words, when will you sway toward energy and effort and say "yes" to a request or choose to respond to a perceived injustice or wrongdoing, and when will you lean toward setting limits for yourself and say "no" as you come to a place where you may find solace in acceptance, surrender, and peace?

---

[1] In 2007, Schwartz co-wrote the article "Manage your energy, not your time" for the *Harvard Business Review* with Catharine McCarthy; it is a good summary of some of the ideas expressed in this book.

FOCUS BOX: THE MEDICINE WHEEL

There is a striking parallel between Loehr and Schwartz's concept of energy and a common framework that has been shared among Indigenous communities for centuries: *the medicine wheel.* According to my friend and colleague Rick McLean, professor of Indigenous studies at Mohawk College, although this concept varies among different Indigenous communities, our whole being is composed of the following four elements: physical, mental (cognitive), emotional, and spiritual. For us to be healthy and live well, we must be in balance by giving equal attention to these four facets of ourselves. If we refrain from adequately doing so, we will be out of balance, and our health and well-being will be adversely impacted. Further, our whole being is intricately interconnected with the land and our relationship with others. An exploration of the medicine wheel and its inherent complexity is beyond the scope of this book, but one that I have been exploring more recently as I deepen my understanding of Indigenous ways of knowing and being. I invite you to learn more as well.

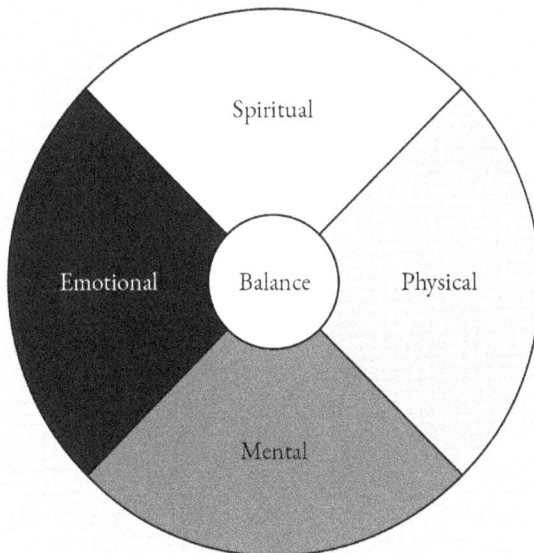

Source: Adapted from Indigenous Fellowship of Hamilton Road (n.d.)

bendABILITY

When I first came up with the term bendABILITY after completing my certificate in applied positive psychology with Emiliya Zhivotovskaya in 2014, it referred to my intention of creating more flexible minds and bodies with the science of positive psychology. Over time, this concept evolved and broadened for me. For our purposes, bendABILITY is a *moment-by-moment choice of if and when to bend and exert energy and effort.* It is the flexibility to lean toward effort when applied to endeavours that are meaningful to us and spark joy, and that we can influence or control, or to move toward setting limits or acceptance and surrender when what we confront is not meaningful to us and is outside our ability to influence or control. Our primary goal in life is to focus our energy and efforts on the first kind of endeavours and then learn to accept and surrender to the rest.

When faced with various propositions, I come back to his basic question: *Is this how I want to spend my energy?* Even "positive" activities have a cost, or an "energy price tag." Many of the things I do are meaningful to me, and I will continue to contribute and/or volunteer my time in pursuit of activities that are aligned with my values and purpose. Sometimes the energy cost is well worth it … and just as I spend my energy engaging in the activity, my tank is replenished with respect to what I get back. Knowing that my actions have an impact on another human being is my greatest motivator. Over the years, I have learned to be choosy when deciding how to spend this coveted currency of my time, energy, and effort.

We may also find ourselves in situations of perceived injustices or wrongdoings, but not every challenging situation deserves our energy and effort. In each moment, we must determine if we want to spend our energy by responding in some way. Timing is also an important factor to consider. If we decide to respond, should we do so immediately, or can we benefit from a pause to gain perspective and space in a situation? What will this response look like? Responding when angry is associated with a higher energy price tag, and dealing with the potential aftermath can have a higher cost too! There are many microdecisions involved in action or inaction. Reflecting on these questions and options requires energy, so put your arms around it. Protect and renew this invaluable resource that fuels every part of you.

Creating Space

Another theme throughout this book is one of *creating space* in our minds and hearts. Sometimes a challenging situation may look quite different later or from another perspective. Although my initial reaction may come from interpreting a situation in a particular way (e.g., "They meant to hurt me," "They are so ignorant for thinking that!") and believing dichotomies (right/wrong, good/bad, etc.), I have learned to approach situations in front of me with a curious mind and open heart[2], creating some much-needed space around a thought, story, and/or emotion. There are multiple ways to see a situation, and I have benefitted from adopting a "maybe not" mindset. I often ask myself a question posed by the beloved Buddhist monk Thích Nhất Hạnh (1999): *"Are you sure?"* Am I 100% confident that there is no other way to interpret the situation in front of me? One of my core beliefs is that we are good people doing the best we can (and sometimes we screw up). But we have choices in how we respond when we have been hurt, or when we have contributed to someone else's hurt. Attempting to act from a place of kindness is important to me, because it is impossible to know what someone else may be going through. In these moments, when contemplating what to do next, I ask myself, "How do I want to exert my energy and effort?" We all make this choice, but for many individuals this response may not be perceived as a choice. This way of moving through the world may not be the right one for all, and a different approach is needed at times for some individuals. This softer approach is one that has brought the most calm and peace to my life. I will continue to make mistakes, to learn, to forgive myself and others, and to make amends when needed. Ultimately, I hope we can approach ourselves and each other in a more mindful way. Given the many stressors in the world and increasingly polarizing views and disconnect among friends, family members, and communities, I believe that a more open and curious approach, where we can operate from a place of spaciousness and kindness, is needed today more than ever.[3]

I also aim to create space when working with challenging emotions that may arise from critical inner dialogue with ourselves. These thoughts and

---

[2] This concept of an open/curious mind and open heart is one that has been shared by several Buddhist meditation teachers including, but not limited to, Thích Nhất Hạnh, Pema Chödrön, Thubten Chodron, Tsoknyi Rinpoche, and Sharon Salzberg.

[3] This point about choice can sometimes reveal our privilege. For example, if you are from a dominant group, you may have the choice to speak up if you notice an injustice. Unfortunately, many individuals who are marginalized in various ways may not have this choice as they need to use their voice to speak up against repeated injustice. As individuals that benefit from this place of privilege, you will need to decide how you want to use it in your daily life. Regardless of how you come into this social justice work (from a place of necessity or privilege), use the tools in this book to take care of yourself as you engage in the emotional labour of this work, and surround yourself with a supportive community. Although I have chosen to use my voice in this way, I acknowledge that it can be exhausting at times, which is why I am committed to promoting self-care for individuals working in this space.

beliefs, including the themes of shame and blame toward self and/or others can intensify our emotional experience. Can we create a more spacious container to hold these emotions? By approaching our emotional landscape with mindfulness and compassion, can we skillfully ride the wave of an edgy emotion, at least some of the time (easier said than done)? *Open heart, open mind.* Can we allow ourselves to feel the anxiety, sadness, or anger *and* make room for joy, peace, and ease? In the upcoming chapters, I will provide helpful tools to navigate these emotional experiences, such as using breath and/or reciting compassionate phrases that highlight impermanence and reinforce our worthiness: "This too shall pass," "Ride the wave," and "I am enough." Building on these concepts of mindfulness and compassion, we weave a different story for ourselves, one that allows for spaciousness and curiosity.

MY INTENTION FOR WRITING THIS BOOK

The goal of this book is to create an experiential exercise for the reader so decisions can be made about where energy and effort are spent. Questions include:

- *What are the things that you can versus cannot control?* Most things in our lives are beyond our control. Much of the distress we experience comes from believing we can control things that we can't (e.g., what others think about us, what others choose to do, the outcomes of our actions). In the words of Viktor Frankl, "When we are no longer able to change a situation, we are challenged to change ourselves."

- *What is the conversation you have with yourself?* What thoughts get in the way of feeling how you want to feel? Some distressful thoughts are that mistakes are to be avoided and that we are not good enough. Everyone makes mistakes; it does not mean that you are flawed. Our mistakes can propel us forward; making them is how we learn.

- *What are your values?* What is really important to you? An internet search will provide you with numerous lists of core values, including but not limited to authenticity, compassion, creativity, fairness, honesty, kindness, love, and spirituality. Which of these, or other values, resonate with you? Reflect on whether your current behaviours align with your values. Being clear on what you stand for will inform the many choices you will make in your life, including how you want to spend your time, energy, and effort. Live your values, as you allow them to be your guide in life.

- *What are your strengths?* In this book, you will be encouraged to explore your unique strengths profile. Can you list some of your strengths? Alternatively, can you list some of your "weaknesses," or lesser strengths? Is it possible that some of your "weaknesses" are your strengths being used in excess or not being applied in an inappropriate context? Learn how you can harness your strengths and apply them in new ways in your life so that you can enhance your life satisfaction, your work, and your interactions.

- *What is your purpose (your why)?* What motivates you to get up in the morning? Reflecting on your values and strengths can help you determine the direction in which you want to move in your life. Ask yourself: What kind of friend/colleague/parent/caregiver do I want to be? What impact do I want to have in my relationships and in my home and work environments? Discover your *ikigai*, a Japanese concept that translates to "our reason for being," as you aim for pursuits that are often greater than you.

By reflecting on your answers to these questions, and others that I will pose throughout this book, I hope that you will expend your energy and effort toward finding a clear direction in your life—one that aligns with your values and strengths.

How is this book different from other Positive Psychology books out there?

This book will explore the science of positive psychology. I will reference various resources to further explore these topics. I encourage you to continue this learning journey after you have finished reading.

By learning more about yourself, I hope you will acknowledge your place in the world, your personal history and experiences, your biases, and possible privilege. There may be parts that you want to avoid, but as I say in my classes, the real learning and growth happens when we are willing to *get comfortable being uncomfortable*. Be brave and do the work. Be curious for the journey ahead.

In addition to the experiential/introspective/reflective parts of this book, I will introduce you to the science of positive psychology and offer you WOW (**W**ays of **O**ptimizing **W**ell-Being) tips to encourage you to create a meaningful and purposeful life. These WOW tips will be organized into three categories: body, mind, and beyond me.

- *Body:* highlights the importance of the body to well-being by practicing and prioritizing body-based exercises like sleep and exercise.

- *Mind:* offers cognitive strategies to identify and challenge thinking patterns and biases that become barriers to personal wellness. Mindfulness, gratitude, and self-compassion are some of the topics that are featured in this section.

- *Beyond Me:* highlights the importance of social connections and purpose, and reflecting on something greater than you.

Goal Setting and Achieving will help you make changes. Often the challenge isn't the *knowing* (e.g., the benefits of sleep, exercise, mindfulness, gratitude), but the *doing.* Your life is an accumulation of your moment-to-moment decisions: what you choose to pursue and what you choose not to. I hope you direct your limited energy to what matters most to you, as this is a book that requires *doing.* Be open, curious, and *bendABLE.*

PART I:
FOUNDATIONS

In this chapter, we will explore the science of positive psychology, the foundation of the rest of the book, and examine the deep relationship between our minds and bodies (the mind-body connection).

POSITIVE PSYCHOLOGY
A Brief History

Positive psychology has roots in some of the early writing of the Greeks. Aristotle exclaimed that "happiness is the meaning and purpose of life, the whole aim and end of human existence." Unfortunately, for most of the 20th century, psychology has emphasized the negative within the framework of the disease model. The focus during this period was on weakness and deficiency—what is wrong with us. As researchers and practitioners were identifying various psychological disorders (to be included in the DSM, the *Diagnostic and Statistical Manual of Mental Disorders* published by the American Psychiatric Association), the goal of psychology became one of finding a cure and relief from these mental health issues. In the 1950s, a new perspective was emerging. Humanistic psychology, led by Abraham Maslow and Carl Rogers, began to challenge some of the views of psychoanalysis (yes, Freud!) and the behaviourists at the time. They offered a more positive view of human nature, with reference to concepts such as free will and self-actualization. Interestingly, it was Maslow who first coined the term "positive psychology" in his book *Toward a Positive Psychology* (1954, as cited in Joseph, 2014). But Martin Seligman is associated with the more recent positive psychology movement. Many in the community refer to him as the father of modern positive psychology. Although he had a background and interest in depression research, as he studied learned helplessness for years, he altered his research interests during his years as the president of the American Psychological Association. In that role, in 1998 his call to action was to turn our attention to the positive, and to focus on topics such as happiness,[4] well-being, optimism, and strengths. He challenged us to ponder the question, "What contributes to a good life?". Along with like-minded colleagues including Christopher Peterson, Mihaly Csikszentmihalyi, Barbara Fredrickson, and Ed Deiner, among others, he launched this new area of study. Seligman's contributions to the field

---

[4] For ease and simplicity, happiness and well-being are used interchangeably throughout this book, although I acknowledge the research that these are distinct yet interrelated concepts. Flourishing is a third related term that is referenced as well, albeit less frequently.

include the concepts of learned optimism, the PERMA model,[5] and character strengths and virtues (this latter topic, character strengths and virtues, was a collaborative effort with Peterson). His colleagues and others began their exploration in these factors that led to a good life … and the field exploded!

What is Positive Psychology?

"Positive psychology is the scientific study of optimal human functioning. It aims to discover and promote the factors that allow individuals and communities to thrive" (Sheldon et al., 1999), or flourish. It is about building what is right with you, rather than fixing what is wrong. And when crap happens (because it will!), it is about giving ourselves "permission to be human" (Ben-Shahar, 2007).

Positive psychology acknowledges several truths:

1. We Are Wired for Emodiversity

> *If there are no ups and downs in your life,*
> *it means you are dead.*

> ~ Author unknown

As humans, we experience a host of emotions throughout life. Although many of us will categorize some of our emotions as *positive* or *good* (e.g., joy, love) and others as *negative* or *bad* (e.g., sadness, anger, anxiety), we should refrain from doing so. Given the range of experiences we will encounter, *all* these emotions are adaptive, and they make sense given what is in front of us. *Emodiversity,* "the variety and relative abundance of the emotions that humans experience," is what is ideal (Newman, 2014; Quoidbach et al., 2014). According to Quoidbach and his colleagues (2014), only experiencing "positive" emotions is not optimal, although on surface it would appear to be, because it lacks authenticity. They posit that "a wide variety of emotions might be a sign of a self-aware and authentic life; such emotional self-awareness and authenticity have been repeatedly linked to health and well-being." Imagine

---

[5] The acronym PERMA stands for Positive emotions, Engagement, Relationships, Meaning, and Accomplishment/Achievement. According to Seligman (2012), in his book *Flourish*, these are the five elements of a flourishing life. Emiliya Zhivotovskaya, founder of the Flourishing Center in NYC and my teacher of positive psychology (I obtained my certificate in applied positive psychology in 2014) added a sixth component with her PERMA-V model, Vitality, to recognize the imperative role of the body in our well-being.

not experiencing sadness when a close friend or relative has passed, or *not* experiencing anger when someone has intentionally hurt you or you have experienced a racial injustice? Anger can motivate us to speak up and advocate for change. Anxiety can motivate us to move toward our goals and help keep us safe. Interestingly, even the rumination that often accompanies depression can be adaptive, as it can aid with the problem-solving process and provide necessary insights (Andrews & Thomson, 2009). These emotions are natural and adaptive when not expressed in extreme form or preventing us from functioning and living the kind of life we want to live. Hutson (2015), in his article "Beyond Happiness: The Upside of Feeling Down," highlights some of the advantages of experiencing some of these emotions (illustrated in Table 1).

TABLE 1: ADVANTAGES OF VARIOUS EMOTIONS

Anxiety	makes us aware of potential threats (keeps us safe), encourages self-discipline
Guilt, embarrassment	makes us reconsider past mistakes and perhaps make amends, and avoid future mistakes
Anger	seeks justice, prevents exploitation
Sadness	focuses our thinking, signals to others that we need help
Envy	makes us strive to better ourselves, have persistence
Regret, disappointment	motivates us to do better next time (learning opportunity), make amends, keeps us out of future trouble

Growth happens when we start *getting comfortable being uncomfortable*. Many of us try to push down our pain and uncomfortable emotions. One downside of this strategy is best expressed in the words of Brené Brown (2010), shame and vulnerability researcher and TED Talk phenom: "We cannot selectively numb emotions, when we numb the painful emotions, we also numb the positive emotions." The aim of positive psychology is not to rid you of uncomfortable emotions, but to provide you with tools so you can move through and not get stuck in them. Pay particular attention to *WOW Tip 5: Cultivate Mindfulness* and *WOW Tip 9: Practice Self-Compassion* to learn how to ride the waves of these uncomfortable and sometimes distressing emotions.

I have highlighted the importance of experiencing "challenging" emotions. Are there also benefits to experiencing "positive" emotions (including love, serenity, forgiveness, awe, joy, interest, hope, pride, amusement, and inspiration), in terms of our physical and psychological health, creativity, productivity, and relationship satisfaction? According to Barbara Fredrickson, author of the book *Positivity* (2009), the answer is yes.[6] In her "broaden-and-build" model (Fredrickson, 2004), positive emotions *broaden* our "thought-action repertoire," and allow us to *build* our intellectual, physical, social, and psychological resources. By doing so, she says, we are better equipped to handle distressing circumstances now *and* later as we create *upward spirals* in our lives.

According to Fredrickson (2011), experiencing positive emotions is associated with a host of benefits. For example, positive emotions open our minds, and we are more likely to see the big picture as we engage in holistic processing. We are more creative, generating more ideas when brainstorming, and we become more resilient as we are better able to bounce back from adversity. Academic performance is enhanced, doctors engage in better medical decision-making, and relationships are strengthened (Fredrickson, 2011). Interestingly, positive emotions can also lead to a longer life. In one study by Danner and her colleagues (2001), young nuns in the 1930s were asked to write a short autobiography. Later, these autobiographies were scored for inclusion of positive, negative, and neutral words. Researchers found a strong positive correlation between inclusion of positive words and longevity; the higher the number of positive words, the longer one tended to live! One of the strengths of this study was the homogeneity of this population, in terms of their diet and lifestyle.

2. We Are Wired To Worry

One of the basic phenomena highlighted in psychology is the *negativity bias*, "the bad is stronger than the good." We pay more attention to the negative compared to the positive. From an evolutionary perspective, this makes sense because this bias is adaptive. If our ancestors ignored the things in their environment that could harm them, there could be serious and sometimes fatal consequences. Our ancestors who survived were cautious and worried.

---

[6] In her book *Positivity*, Fredrickson claimed that to flourish, we need to experience at least three positive emotions to offset the one challenging emotion we experience (a 3:1 positivity ratio). Since its publication, Brown and his colleagues (2013) wrote an article claiming that there were errors in the mathematical equation used to derive this 3:1 positivity ratio. In response to this critique, Fredrickson (2013) agreed that the model was inaccurate. Despite these inaccuracies, her claim that higher positivity ratios are predictive of well-being and other beneficial outcomes (within bounds) has been substantiated by numerous researchers over the years.

They reacted by attacking the threat or escaping the situation—the fight-or-flight response in action. Today, we are not dealing with periodic threats from our environments but chronic stress, and our bodies pay a heavy price because this process is no longer adaptive. Throughout this book, strategies to better cope with the stressors in our lives will be offered. Can a stressor be reframed? Are there adoptable strategies that can lower the amount of stress experienced? There is nothing inherently wrong with stress or how our bodies react to it. In fact, we should be thankful when we become reactive, because our bodies are doing exactly what they were built to do—keep us safe.

3. We Are Wired for Connection

We are social animals, and we have evolved to belong to groups. But over time, we have disconnected from these essential social networks. We are the loneliest generation, and evidence shows that loneliness is impacting our mental health, with increasing rates of anxiety and depression, as well as our physical well-being. In *WOW Tip 14: Foster Connection*, we will explore the importance of our relationships to our wellness (think about it: there's an "I" in "illness" and a "we" in "wellness"), and how zooming out of our personal realm and investing in these relationships can increase our sense of well-being.

What are the reasons for these feelings of disconnection and loneliness? There are several factors, including one that we can't ignore: technology. There are many advantages and conveniences associated with devices, like connecting with people we care about. It is *how* we use our devices—time spent on social media, perfecting profiles, consuming inaccurate images and "facts," seeking approval with thumbs-ups and likes—and our excessive use that can be problematic. Consider *"phubbing,"* or phone snubbing. Have you ever ignored someone to check your phone? Has this happened to you? I've had several discussions on this topic, and reactions have varied from "It's no big deal" to "It's extremely rude or insensitive," but what is being communicated by this behaviour is the most important question. As the recipient, do you feel worthy? Do you feel respected? How does this behaviour impact the quality of relationships, and does it create distance? Additional consequences of misusing or overusing technology are documented in the research literature, and span several categories (including physical, cognitive, emotional, and relationship). In *WOW Tip 11: Create a New Relationship with Your Tech Devices,* we will further explore our relationship with technology and its potential impacts on various areas of functioning and on personal relationships.

What Contributes to Well-Being?

A SHORT QUIZ

1. In general, are people living in California happier than people living in the Midwest?

2. In general, are lottery winners happier than people with paraplegia?

3. Does money buy happiness?

4. In general, are individuals who go to church happier than those who do not?

5. In general, are parents happier than those individuals without children?

6. Does hanging out with happier people lead to a boost in happiness?

(answers begin on page 18)

In 2005, Sonya Lyubomirsky, author of the books *The How of Happiness* and *The Why of Happiness*, and fellow researchers Kennon Sheldon and David Schkade wrote a seminal paper that referenced the "Happiness Pie" (Figure 1). They highlighted three factors that affect our happiness level: genetics/set point (50%), life circumstances (10%), and intentional activities (40%); the number in parentheses is the percentage of the variance within a population (that is, at the group level; these percentages do not apply at the individual level, where 50% of *my* happiness may be determined by genetics). This finding led the researchers and positive psychology scientists to be optimistic about one's ability to change their happiness/well-being. Although genetics accounted for the biggest chunk of this variance (we cannot change who our parents are), we do have control and can make different choices with respect to our intentional activities such as gratitude exercises, meditation practice, and exercise. Further, life circumstances had the smallest impact on our overall happiness level (10%). This was an interesting observation, because many of us put much effort into changing our life circumstances, such as getting an education, finding a job, or buying/renting a home. Although these pursuits can influence our happiness and well-being, gaining titles and resources

FIGURE 1: THE HAPPINESS PIE

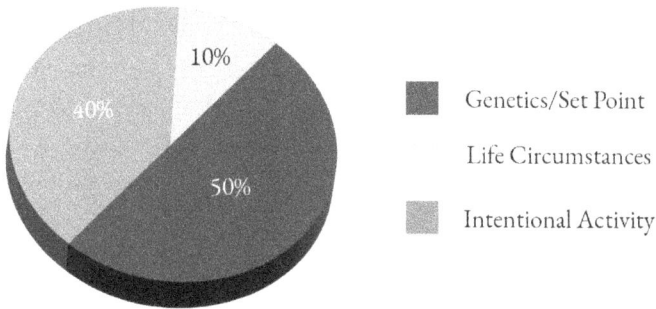

Genetics/Set Point

Life Circumstances

Intentional Activity

Source: Adapted from Lyubomirsky et al. (2005)

have less of an impact than we believe (Lyubomirsky et al., 2005). Since the publication of the original paper, some researchers have raised critiques about the model, specifically the weights of these three factors (50/40/10). Sheldon and Lyubomirsky (2019) addressed these concerns and agreed with many of the critiques. They concluded that although the approximate percentages were not accurate, the overall takeaways still applied. Individuals can engage in deliberate efforts and activities to increase their happiness, but the impact of these efforts is much smaller than originally reported (less than 40%). Subsequent research suggests that the heritability component accounts for a bigger slice of the pie at 54%, and a slightly higher estimate of 61% of the variance is cited if the studies in question were weighted for their sample sizes (Brown & Rohrer, 2020, 2021). This latter point may seem discouraging, especially if you believe that your happiness set point is lower on the scale. We don't come into the world as blank slates. (Sorry, John Locke, but your tabula rasa theory is wrong!) Some of us need to work harder to experience happiness. Putting in the work can pay off, as there are things that we can do to shift this biological set point. What we choose to do and how we think is mostly under our control, and we experience fluctuations to our happiness every day. What do you do right now that brings you peace, well-being, and/ or happiness? For additional ideas, jump to the *WOW* section of this book!

Although I support this narrative, I do not want to minimize the impact of our life circumstances and experiences. Applying the wellness tips that are shared throughout this book can nudge us toward a more flourishing experience, but these interventions may be less helpful if one cannot reliably access safe housing, a secure income, or healthy food/clean water, and if experiences of systemic racism or other forms of discrimination and oppression are part of their reality. Over several decades, research has shown that broader systemic and material variables, including the social determinants of health, are crucial factors that influence our physical and psychological well-being. So why are these factors often missing or minimized in some positive psychology research? Reasons include the focus of some of this research, with an overemphasis on internal, psychological factors, and overreliance on quantitative and survey research that asks closed-ended questions on a narrow array of topics. By broadening one's research scope, studying this topic with a more contextual lens, and utilizing qualitative methodologies such as ethnographies, these other key variables surface. In a recent research study, anthropologist Sara Willen and her colleagues (2021) conducted interviews with a diverse group of participants in the Ohio area. They found that the likelihood that a person reported they were flourishing or at least leaning in this direction (65% of their community members sample) differed across key demographic variables. As illustrated in Figure 2, participants who were women, older, white, highly educated, and earning a higher income were more likely to report flourishing.

FIGURE 2: PERCENT FLOURISHING (YES/LEANS YES) BY DEMOGRAPHIC GROUP

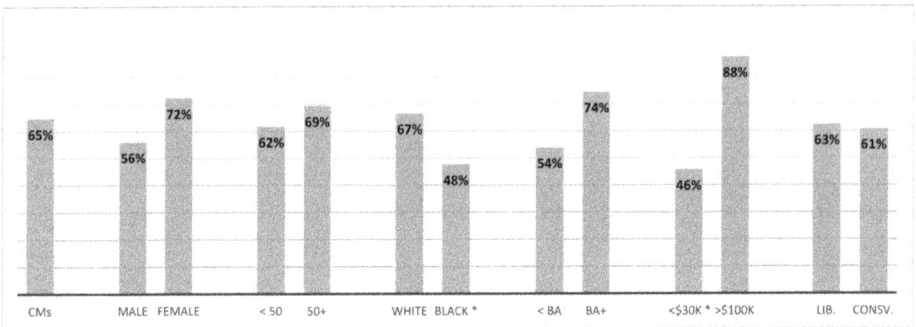

Note: * statistically significant difference (p<0.05); "CMs" refers to "community members"

Source: Willen et al. (2021)

Participants were asked to share the top three things that lead individuals to flourish. As Figure 3 illustrates, social support, a stable income, and the social determinants of health highlight these broader contextual factors beyond the individual;[7] the latter two, specifically, emphasize these structural and material influences (Willen et al., 2021).

---

[7] According to Willen and her colleagues (2021), the social determinants of health include "access to food, housing, transportation, and education; neighborhood and physical environment; sense of safety; government institutions; exposure to the police/justice system; discrimination; and structural oppression."

FIGURE 3: TOP FACTORS AFFECTING FLOURISHING

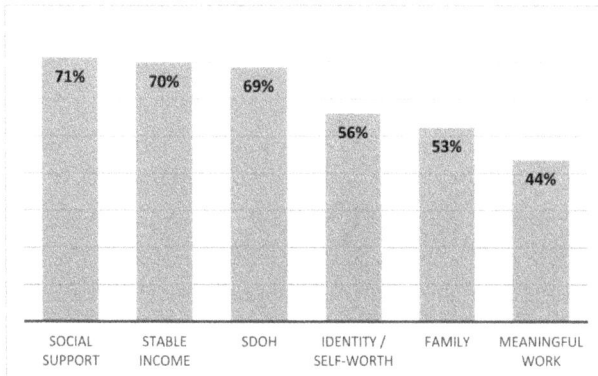

Source: Willen et al. (2021)

The researchers gathered rich stories and experiences from their participants. They shared samples from their collection that demonstrate the complex and dynamic interplay between factors at the individual and societal levels, and how our (in)ability to access social determinants of health have a significant impact on our sense of well-being. For example, a woman in her 50s emphasized the importance of what she calls a "healthy home":

> Because your home is your sanctuary .... But if you have a home that's falling apart, ... that's infested with roaches, and mold, and, and lead, and ... water coming in, and then after you've worked so hard, and then you come home and you just want to rest, and then you're like oh I don't have food, and, ... it's raining; oh now we got to put you know, buckets here ... there we go, mice again. ... you cannot rest ... So now your health is going out of whack. You get depressed, mental issues. Violence, because you're angry .... because Ah! Why do I have to live life like this? And Ah! Why can't I pay for this? Why can't I get—why can't the landlord fix this? ... So you're not being a good mom because you're angry. So you didn't even want to talk to your kids ... you didn't want to cook ... So then you're eating unhealthy. So you're creating all these negative environments. So it's mental health, stress, ...so you cannot give 100% at home. So if you cannot give 100% at home, you cannot give 100% to work, and you cannot give 100% to social life, and you have no friends, because you're so angry nobody wants to talk to you. So for me, it's very important that you have a healthy home.

One unfortunate interpretation of positive psychology research is that the bulk of what determines our happiness is within our control. I have sometimes left these positive psychology-related talks and seminars with the "fluffy" and naive message that if we want to feel better, we only need to think differently and practice some wellness interventions. *You can do it!* Although this message may resonate for many readers of this book, it falls flat for others, especially if their needs for safety, security, and belonging have not been met. Will a gratitude exercise help if you are worried about putting food on your table? Please keep this in mind as you experiment and share the interventions that are offered throughout this book. Although these interventions can be helpful, sometimes structural and systemic changes need to take place so that we can collectively access resources and opportunities that will impact our well-being.

Back to the quiz at the start of this subsection:

Before I provide the answers to these questions, I want to highlight two well-documented observations:

1. Many of us do not know what brings us happiness.

2. We are not very good at predicting how events will affect us, for better or worse, in the future.

So why do we get it wrong much of the time? One reason is the *focusing illusion*, our tendency to focus on one aspect of our lives to the exclusion of other important aspects (Schkade & Kahneman, 1998). Unfortunately, because of messages we have received from our families, friends, and the media, we often focus on the *wrong* things. With this in mind, let us turn our attention to the answers to the quiz.

(✗) *In general, are people living in California happier than people living in the Midwest?* No.

FACT: There is no significant difference in happiness levels between Californians and Midwesterners. In Schkade and Kahneman's (1998) study, they found that most people wrongfully assumed that individuals who live in California are happier than those who live in the Midwest. The climate factor appears to loom large in individuals' incorrect predictions, the researchers found. Focusing on climate and minimizing the importance of factors that have a stronger association with well-being such as relationships, meaningful work, and leisure activities—factors that are the same in these two settings—leads one to make this predictive error (Schkade & Kahneman, 1998). Marketing companies exploit this cognitive bias when advertising to us. By making us feel that we *need* to own their product to feel happy, we are more likely to buy it. If we feel a temporary boost from our purchase, this momentary happiness is short-lived thanks to hedonic adaptation; more on this concept below.

(X) *In general, are lottery winners happier than people with paraplegia?*
No.

FACT: Following a pivotal event such as winning the lottery or having an accident resulting in paraplegia, people with paraplegia are only slightly less happy than lottery winners, but most people predicted that there would be a significant difference in happiness/well-being between the two groups (Brickman et al., 1978). Research over the years in *affective forecasting* has consistently demonstrated that we are terrible at predicting how positive or negative events will impact us. Brickman and his colleagues (1978) found that although individuals experienced the expected rise/drop in their happiness level immediately after winning the lottery or experiencing paraplegia, in contrast to participants' predictions, those living with paraplegia were only slightly less happy at a future date than the lottery winners. Buying a new house or getting a new job does make us happier, but we adapt and return to baseline as we chase our next purchase or goal. Likewise, experiencing a life-altering event, such as losing a physical ability, has a negative impact on our well-being, at least in the short-term. In the long-term, we adapt, and our happiness returns to pre-accident levels. We are more resilient than we think, and there is growing evidence in post-traumatic growth research that demonstrates this (we will explore this topic in further detail in *WOW Tip 7: Make Meaning as You Create Empowering Stories*). These observations align with our understanding of *hedonic adaptation/ hedonic treadmill*, a concept described by Brickman and Campbell (1971) and illustrated in Figure 4, whereby we return to our happiness set point after experiencing something positive or negative.

As Kahneman (2013) has stated, "Nothing in life is as important as you think it is when you're thinking about it." We overestimate how much joy we will obtain by making a material purchase or attaining a goal, and how long our mood boost will last. And likewise, we underestimate our resiliency when unfortunate events happen. Can we remember this fluctuation in our happiness/well-being the next time we find ourselves in a challenging situation? Can we zoom out so the event/emotion benefits from a clearer perspective? With time, we will likely bounce back and return to our happiness set point level. And when good things happen, savour the experience, because this is unlikely to last as we adapt again. We will visit this concept of impermanence, the idea that nothing lasts forever, in future chapters.

FIGURE 4: HEDONIC ADAPTATION

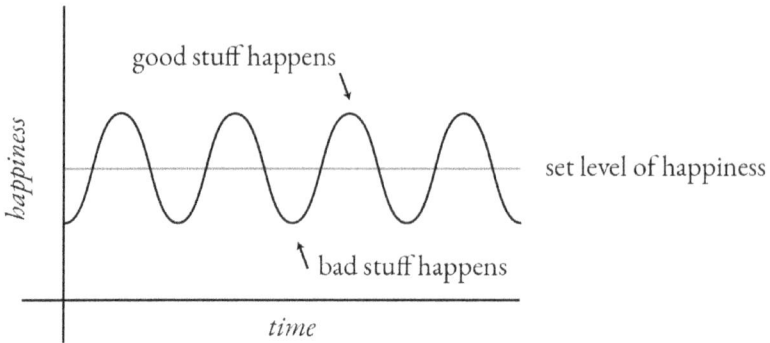

Source: Adapted from a figure cited in Schaffner (2016)

✓ *Does money buy happiness?*
Yes … sort of!

FACT: New research by Killingsworth (2021) shows a positive correlation between money (indicated by household income) and happiness. As demonstrated in Figure 5, "experienced and evaluative well-being increased linearly with log(income) with an equally steep slope for higher earners as for lower earners" (Killingsworth, 2021). This study measured two types of well-being (WB) using the author's *Track Your Happiness* app in which participants were asked to rate their WB periodically throughout the day at random intervals:

- *Experienced WB*: real-time feeling reports (i.e., How do you feel *right now?* Response endpoints ranged from "very bad" to "very good")

- *Evaluative WB*: overall life satisfaction (i.e., Overall, how satisfied are you with your life? Response endpoints ranged from "not at all" to "extremely")

This research contrasts with research by Kahneman and Deaton (2010), who reported that overall there is little correlation between happiness levels and financial wealth. They found that positive affect rises with log income up to $75,000 (US dollars). Money contributes to happiness, they concluded, but only when the added wealth ensures stability (e.g., putting food on the table or securing safe housing). Beyond this point, money did not appear to continue to contribute to our well-being, at least to the upper limit of wealth observed in this study.

FIGURE 5: MEAN LEVELS OF EXPERIENCED WELL-BEING AND EVALUATIVE WELL-BEING FOR EACH INCOME BAND.

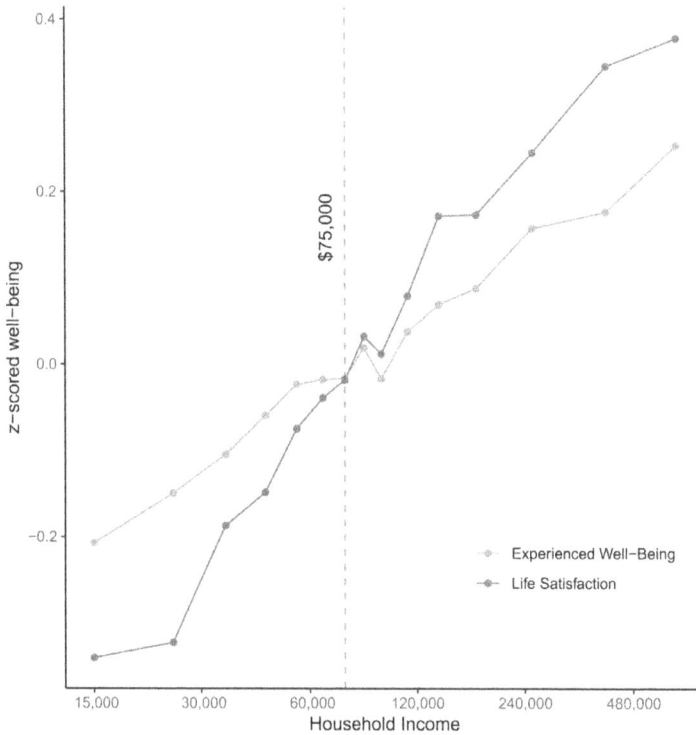

Note: Income axis is log transformed.

Source: Killingsworth (2021)

Before prioritizing money, there are a few caveats to highlight:

- Remember that this is correlational data, and it does not mean causation. Although this finding is often interpreted as money *leads to* happiness, it is also possible that people who are already happier make more money, among other explanations.

- We need to highlight how the variables were represented on the x- and y-axes of Figure 5 above (Note: Even Kahneman and Deaton's 2010 study plotted wealth in this way). For example, household income was plotted on a log scale (i.e., each point along this axis doubles). So, as income increases, well-being increases at a slower rate, so that a particular sum of money (e.g., $10,000), has a greater impact on someone earning $20,000 per year compared to someone earning $200,000 per year. In fact, a person's $20,000 income doubling to

$40,000 would have the same increase in happiness, on average, as another person's $100,000 income doubling to $200,000!

Chasing money isn't a good goal when it comes to happiness. In fact, desiring wealth leaves one *less* happy (Kasser, 2002, as cited in Boniwell, 2012). Killingsworth (2021) cautioned readers of his study to not make earning more money a priority. He reported that people who "defined their personal success in terms of money ... tended on average to be less happy ... you want to have it, but you want to not care too much about it" (as cited in Enten, 2022).

What seems to be more important than the amount of money you have is how you spend it:

1. *Spend Your Money on Experiences Versus Material Goods.*

Spending money this way increases one's happiness. Thomas Gilovich and his colleagues (2015) cite numerous studies to support this recommendation. Further, they propose three mechanisms to explain why experiential purchases are associated with increased happiness and are more immune to hedonic adaptation—in other words, the boost in happiness lasts longer. One of the mechanisms to highlight is that experiential purchases such as going to the theatre often involve social interaction. Research shows that social connection is imperative to one's happiness and well-being. On the flipside, prioritizing material purchases often impedes our happiness. Research demonstrates that people who are materialistic are in fact less happy. This is indicated by the experience of more challenging emotions and lower scores on relatedness, autonomy, competence, gratitude, and meaning in life (Kashdan & Breen, 2007). Interestingly, one mediating factor in the research is low levels of gratitude in materialistic individuals.

2. *Spend Your Money on Other People Instead of Yourself.*

In a study by Dunn and her colleagues (2008), spending money on others led to a greater boost in happiness than spending money on oneself.

✓ *In general, are individuals who go to church happier than those who do not?* Yes.

FACT: Going to church is linked to being happier and living longer (Ciarrocchi et al., 2008, as cited in Boniwell, 2012). Please note that the research is correlational, meaning that there is a relationship between church attendance and happiness. We cannot assume the directional nature of this relationship (i.e., it could be that attending church causes an increase in happiness, *or* individuals who are already happier are more likely to go to church, or both). Aside from the religious/spiritual aspect of church and one's faith, as well as believing one's life has a higher purpose, going to church also involves socializing and perhaps helping family, friends, and community members.

(X) *In general, are parents happier than those individuals without children?*
No, although it is a complex relationship.

FACT: Having children does not make you happier, and having young kids (under age five) and teens makes you *less* happy (Kobrin & Hendersot, 1977, as cited in Boniwell, 2012). An interesting side note is that parents tend to live longer. An important distinction to make is between a happy life (with respect to hedonic well-being or WB) and a meaningful and purposeful life (eudaemonic WB). Raising children, with its number of joys but also challenges, may not be pleasurable a lot of the time (low hedonic WB), but we can reflect on these important relationships and find meaning in them (high eudaemonic WB). According to Deaton and Stone (2014), despite the observation that parents, compared to nonparents, show greater fluctuations in well-being (more joy *and* daily stress), "If parents choose to be parents, and nonparents choose to be nonparents, there is no reason to expect that one group will be better or worse off than the other once other circumstances are controlled."

(✓) *Does hanging out with happier people lead to a boost in happiness?*
Yes.

FACT: Hanging out with happy people increases one's happiness (Christakis & Fowler, 2009, as cited in Boniwell, 2012). This finding highlights the concept of *emotional contagion*, or "the tendency to automatically mimic and synchronize expressions, vocalizations, postures, and movements with those of another person's and, consequently, to converge emotionally" (Hatfield et al., 1993). There is ample evidence in history, the animal world, across the lifespan, and in clinical settings that emotions are contagious—both "positive" emotions and "negative" emotions. When you spend time with individuals who are cranky, do you start feeling this way as well? One mechanism is that we mimic other people's vocal and non-verbal behaviours and movements without conscious awareness, and we do so shortly after birth. This facial and bodily feedback is often very subtle, and cannot be seen by the naked eye. In one study conducted by Dimberg and Thunberg (1998, as cited in Dimberg et al., 2000), subtle microchanges in the participants' various facial muscles were observed while viewing happy and sad faces after a brief 500-millisecond exposure; they were mimicking the facial expressions they were observing. In subsequent research, this mimicry effect appears to happen at an unconscious level (Dimberg et al., 2000). A word of caution: Consider who you surround yourself with, in social circles and with family, friends, and colleagues. According to Cameron (2008), the *heliotropic effect* is "the tendency in all living systems toward positive energy and away from negative energy." We can see this bias operating with all living systems. Just as plants grow and lean toward the sun, humans lean toward positive energy in others, and benefit from it as they in turn enhance the work of others around them. If you are a manager, invest in and nurture positive energizers—your return on investment will be multiplied! For example, the NBA's Shane Battier may have been an unknown player, but with his "contagious" energy, he was an incredible force when he was on the court. He was known as a positive energizer (Lewis, 2009), as he improved his team's performance, while simultaneously worsening his opponents'.

We are often not aware of what contributes to our happiness and well-being. We chase things in life such as money, material possessions, and status that may not contribute as much as we think to our sense of well-being and may in fact undermine it. There is one factor that I have not discussed thus far: *time affluence*. This is a topic that is receiving increased attention in recent years, especially with the publication of Ashley Whillans's book *Time Smart* (2020). Time affluence is defined as "the state of having and using time meaningfully" (Whillans, 2020). I have devoted much of my career to teaching others how to take care of themselves, encouraging my students to make the time for activities that will contribute to their well-being and happiness. And there I was, on my computer, checking email and just being "busy," never feeling like I had enough time. We will explore this topic of time affluence, and the importance of creating much-needed free space in our lives, in further detail in *WOW Tip 10: Become More Time Affluent*. I will share my tricks and tips with you so that you can direct your limited resources—your energy, your time— into the pursuits that truly matter to you and will enhance your sense of well-being. It's about getting more of what matters done in less time.

MIND-BODY CONNECTION

One area in positive psychology that I am passionate about is the mind-body connection. Namely, the power of neuroplasticity, which is the brain's ability to heal, grow, and reorganize itself, and the many ways in which our bodies influence our minds (such as our perceptions, thoughts, feelings, and judgments), and likewise, our minds influence our bodies, as these seemingly separate "systems" are deeply intertwined. One example of this intricate connection is seen in the many ways trauma resides in our bodies, a viewpoint advanced by Peter Levine (author of *Healing Trauma*), Gabor Maté (author of *When the Body Says No* and *The Myth of Normal*), and Bessel van der Kolk (author of *The Body Keeps the Score*), among others. Tara Brach, in her book *Radical Compassion* (2020a), references this point when she says, "Our issues are in our tissues." This topic is beyond the scope of this book, but I encourage you to further explore these ideas if this topic is of interest to you.

Neuroplasticity

According to Norman Doidge, psychiatrist and author of *The Brain That Changes Itself* (2007) and *The Brain's Way of Healing* (2015), our thoughts and actions can not only alter our brain's anatomy (its structure), but also its physiology (its function). This process is referred to as *neuroplasticity*. Here is some evidence of our brain's incredible ability to reorganize itself.

1. Hemispherectomy

A hemispherectomy is a surgical procedure in which there is a removal of the left or right cerebral hemisphere of the brain. Some may opt for this surgery because of their experience with debilitating seizures that may be localized to one side of the brain, as in the case of Rasmussen syndrome. Many individuals might predict that the consequences of surgery would be substantial: Would they be able to speak, communicate, and move? But contrary to this belief, individuals do remarkably well because the remaining hemisphere takes over some of the function that was once ascribed to the now missing hemisphere. It begins to reorganize itself through the creation of new neurons, or neurogenesis, and the overall rewiring of this neuronal network (Baiyekusi & Prasad, 2016). With the addition of rehabilitative therapies such as Taub's constraint-induced movement therapy (CIMT), where individuals are required to use the affected parts of their body, incredible progress can be seen with repeated practice as the brain learns to reorganize and rewire itself.

2. Taub's Constraint-Induced Movement Therapy (CIMT)

The right side of the brain controls the left side of the body and vice versa. If someone's right side of the brain has been affected in some way, such as a hemispherectomy, or brain injury due to a traumatic accident, stroke, or other causes, one may see some deficits on the left side of the body. Many survivors meet this challenge by compensating with the "good" side of their body. In this case, an individual having difficulty using their left hand may resort to using only their "good" right hand to pick up objects and perform everyday tasks. As a result, the affected left hand will never improve its functioning. In CIMT, an individual is prevented from using their "good" hand by wearing a large mitt, which forces them to pick up blocks, food, and other items with their affected hand. Over time, one can expect to see improved functioning in their affected hand due to the power of neuroplasticity (Taub et al., 2005, as cited in Doidge, 2007).

3. London Cab Drivers

And we could not include a section on neuroplasticity without mentioning the incredible brains of London cab drivers. A study by Maguire and her colleagues (2000) found that their extensive knowledge of the intricate and complicated road system altered these cab drivers' brains, specifically the hippocampal region known for memory formation. Having thousands of hours of experience navigating these roadways literally changed the brains of these seasoned, expert drivers. Their hippocampi were much larger than individuals without this extensive experience. Further, the more experience they had navigating these roads, the greater the growth in this brain region (Maguire et al., 2000).

Diving into the Mind-Body Connection

Ample research shows that interventions aimed at the physical body can generate powerful "mind" benefits (perceptions, thoughts, feelings, and judgments). Strategies targeting the mind can likewise lead to benefits in how our physical bodies function. Although this presentation may make the directional relationship between mind and body appear linear (i.e., body → mind, mind → body), the actual mechanisms underlying these relationships are quite complex and bidirectional in nature.

1. Body to Mind (Embodied Cognition)

A. Power Posing

In 2012, psychologist Amy Cuddy delivered a TED Talk entitled *Your Body Language May Shape Who You Are*. Almost immediately, the video went viral and influenced the way people think about the power of body language. Cuddy shared details of her studies that demonstrated that "power posing"—think about Wonder Woman standing in a confident pose—can alter our body chemistry and our feelings of confidence, as well as impact our probability of success. In her 2015 book *Presence*, she described several studies she conducted with her colleagues on this power posing effect. In one study (Carney et al., 2010), participants were instructed to take either a low-power pose, where the body is constricted, or a high-power pose, expressed in expansive body postures, for a duration of two minutes. Later, their testosterone and cortisol levels were measured, and they found that compared to baseline, the high-power posers experienced an increase in testosterone (T) and a decrease in cortisol (C), our "stress" hormone. The low-power posers showed the opposite pattern ($\downarrow$ T, $\uparrow$ C). Further, the high-power posers reported increased feelings of power. In a subsequent study that used the same manipulation prior to an interview, high-power posers were judged to have increased "presence" during their interview and were more likely to be chosen for hire (Cuddy et al., 2015). Changing one's body, for a mere two minutes, can have dramatic effects on how one feels, in turn impacting how one is perceived by others. It should be noted that some later studies have failed to reliably replicate these findings, especially with respect to the physiological changes in T and C levels underlying this effect.[8]

B. Facial Feedback Hypothesis

Can feedback from our facial muscles influence our emotional experiences? Some studies show that the answer is yes. In one study (Strack et al., 1988), participants were randomly assigned to one of three groups. The first group, the "smile group," was asked to hold a pencil with their teeth. Holding a pencil in between your teeth forces a smile. The second group had to hold the pencil with their lips, generating a neutral facial expression. The third group, the control group, was asked to hold the pencil with their nondominant hand. They were then asked to rate a cartoon. The results indicated that the smile group rated the cartoon as funnier, compared to the other two groups.[9]

Another demonstration of this effect was illustrated in a study by Wollmer (2012, as cited in Rodriguez, 2012). The question was: Is it possible that a Botox injection to one's face can help individuals with depression? The logic was that if a Botox injection made it difficult for a person to frown—Botox patients often state that they have difficulty expressing emotion on their faces—would they in turn experience fewer depressive symptoms? To test this hypothesis, individuals with depression were randomly assigned to two groups. Group 1 received five Botox injections, while group 2 received five injections

---

[8] If you are interested in exploring the criticisms of this study, namely its issue with replicability, they are outlined in a paper by Simmons and Simonsohn (2017) entitled "Power Posing: P-Curving the Evidence." In response, Cuddy and her colleagues (2018) cited a review of 55 studies that found a clear link between power posing and feelings of power, even though the effect of power posing on one's body chemistry was not reliably demonstrated in these studies.

[9] Concerns have been raised about the replicability of this effect. In a meta-analysis of the facial feedback literature, Coles and his colleagues (2019) reported that the effects (if any) are small and variable.

of a placebo. As predicted, the Botox group experienced a reduction of depressive symptoms, more so than the control group. If this study has piqued your interest and you are considering Botox as a "wellness" strategy, you may want to reserve your curiosity and keep reading!

C. Physical and Emotional Warmth Link

There is growing research that suggests that there is a link between physical warmth and psychological warmth (for a summary, see Bargh & Melnikoff, 2019). In fact, the perception of both physical warmth and psychological warmth is linked to a region in the brain called the insula. In a remarkable study, Williams and Bargh (2008) had participants ride in an elevator with the experimenter and hold their coffee ("hot" or "cold"). Later, all participants were asked to rate 10 different people on personality traits. The result of the study was that the "hot" coffee group gave warmer ratings than the "cold" coffee group.[10] Similarly, in a subsequent study in the same paper, participants were asked to rate the effectiveness of therapeutic pads. Some of the participants rated hot pads whereas others rated cold pads, again determined by random assignment. Later they were given a treat and told that they could keep it for themselves or give it to a friend. The result of this study was that the "hot" raters were more likely to give the treat to their friend. These findings suggest that physical warmth promotes kindness, an aspect of psychological warmth.

D. Exercise

The benefits of exercise have been well-documented in the research literature and the media. For example, bursts of movement prior to a test can improve one's performance, and engaging in a regular exercise regimen has been shown to be as effective, if not more effective, as taking psychiatric medications for various mental health issues, including antidepressants and benzodiazepines, among others.[11] John Ratey and his co-author, Erik Hagerman, explore these impacts among others in their book *Spark* (2008). To learn more about the impact of exercise beyond the physical benefits, see

---

[10] Chabris and his colleagues (2019) failed to replicate this finding. In response, Bargh and Melnikoff (2019) addressed their criticisms and highlighted procedural differences between the original study and subsequent replication studies, and offered further evidence of this physical-social warmth pathway. If you are interested in this research, which is beyond the scope of this book, I encourage you to read this latter paper

[11] If you have a prescription for a psychotropic medication, please do not interpret this finding as medical advice to stop taking your prescription. Please consult your doctor and/or healthcare professional for guidance in deciding how to best support your mental health. It could be that a combination of medication and an exercise regimen will be your best course of action. Do not wean yourself off a prescribed medication without medical support and supervision.

WOW Tip 3: Exercise.

2. Mind to Body

   A. Placebo Effect

There is ample research to show that a person's *expectations* that a treatment (e.g., sugar pill, sham surgery) will work often leads to beneficial effects. These benefits can range from improvements in one's mood or anxiety to pain relief. When attempting to explain why, some scholars (see Novella, 2017) refer to placebo effects, because there are several mechanisms that likely underlie these benefits. Aside from reasons that include regression to the mean, bias in perceiving and/or reporting symptoms such as favourable assessments to please one's care provider, and other details of the "treatment" including the relaxing atmosphere and attention from one's care provider, the one we highlight here is that one's *belief* that improvement is possible causes physiological changes in one's body. In fact, the endorphins, our "pain-relieving" endogenous opioid, and dopamine, a neurotransmitter linked to reward-motivated behaviour and pleasure, among other neurotransmitters and hormones, are connected to the placebo effect (Marchant, 2016).

Interestingly, a *nocebo effect* has also been observed in the literature. In this case, if you expect a treatment to produce negative effects or side effects, you may in fact experience them.

   B. Mindfulness

If you are familiar with the growing literature surrounding meditation, you know engaging in regular mindfulness meditation has the potential to change the brain and body in amazing ways. To dive into this research, read *WOW Tip 5: Cultivate Mindfulness.*

   C. View Stress As a Challenge Versus a Threat

When stressed, we experience several physiological changes in our bodies that are part of the "fight-or-flight" response—accelerated heart rate, rapid breathing—or "freeze" response—immobility. The adrenaline-fueled fight-or-flight response results from the activation of the sympathetic nervous system. But under stressful circumstances, is this response inevitable? According to psychologist Kelly McGonigal, author of *The Upside of Stress* and TED Talk speaker (*How to Make Stress Your Friend*), the answer is no. In fact, perceiving a stressful event as a challenge versus a threat can change how we respond to the situation. As she highlights in her TED Talk (McGonigal, 2013), viewing one's stress response as helpful can change how we physiologically respond in our bodies; instead of our blood vessels constricting, they are more likely to stay relaxed. So even if your heart is pounding, having your blood vessels remain relaxed is a healthier cardiovascular response. The next time you are in a stressful situation, say to your body, "Thank you for helping me get ready to cope with the challenge in front of me." If you are perceiving the situation in front of you with a catastrophic lens, go to *WOW Tip 6: Challenge Your Perspective and Mind Chatter* to discover ways you can challenge your perspective and unproductive mind chatter that may not be serving you in that moment.

D. Psychotherapy

Several studies support the fact that changing the way we think can change the brain. Clients that participate in various forms of psychotherapy, including Cognitive Behavioural Therapy (CBT), often show emotional benefits to their mood and anxiety as well as accompanying physiological changes with respect to both brain anatomy and molecular and cellular changes (Karlsson, 2013). In more recent years, mindfulness interventions have been integrated with traditional therapeutic approaches to treat a host of physical and mental health issues, from depression and anxiety to chronic pain and other ailments. Third-wave CBT interventions, including Mindfulness-Based Cognitive Therapy (MBCT), an adaptation of Jon Kabat-Zinn's MBSR program created by Zindel Siegel, Mark Williams, and John Teasdale; Dialectical and Behavioural Therapy (DBT), developed by Marsha Linehan; and Acceptance and Commitment Therapy (ACT), created by Steven Hayes, underscore a mindfulness-based focus to these treatments. All three treatment modalities have shown promise in treating a range of psychological disorders.

PART II:
WOW TIPS

I have subdivided this chapter into three sections: Body, Mind, and Beyond Me. This categorization will help highlight the primary focus of each intervention. For each intervention, you will learn:

- *The What*: What is the concept/intervention?

- *The Why*: What are the benefits of cultivating this practice/ implementing this intervention?

- *The How*: How can one cultivate this practice (experiential component)?

While reading these tips, you may feel compelled to skip the *doing* part of this last section (*The How*). To achieve the most benefits, you are encouraged to pause and complete the exercises.

WOW TIPS:
BODY

In this section, body-based interventions/exercises that are known to increase one's well-being are highlighted. One topic that has close ties with our well-being is our diet. I have not included this topic here as I do not have expertise in this area.

The focus of this section is on the following:

- WOW Tip 1: Breathe

- WOW Tip 2: Sleep

- WOW Tip 3: Exercise

- WOW Tip 4: Practice Self-Care

WOW TIP 1:
BREATHE

THE WHAT & WHY

Is it better to be a nose breather or a mouth breather? Or is air getting into your lungs the only thing that matters? What about the pace of breathing? Are you taking too many breaths during your day? Many people breathe through their mouths and take too many breaths throughout the day; this is shown to be problematic for their overall health. In this section, I will highlight evidence of the benefits of breathing through the nose, slowing down the pace of breath, and extending exhalations. For more information, you may be interested in reading James Nestor's book *Breath* (2020).

Tip 1: Breathe through your nose.

Yes, it matters *how* we breathe! When we breathe through our nose, the ingested air goes through a filtering process before it reaches our lungs. The air is heated, moistened, and then filtered, first by nasal hairs that act as a screen to collect pollens and allergens, and then by the mucous and cilia, hair-like filters higher in the nasal cavity that collect other pollutants and bacteria. The nose releases nitric oxide, a vasodilator that helps to widen bloods vessels and improve oxygen circulation within the body. Together, the filtered air moves to the lungs and then is more easily absorbed into the bloodstream. Nestor (2020) points out that we can "extract 20% more oxygen breathing through our noses than we can equivalent breaths through our mouths." By breathing like this, there can be beneficial effects on performance, especially endurance, in addition to improved sleep, relaxation, and better physical and mental health. Mouth breathing, where unfiltered air goes directly to the lungs, can have detrimental health effects on blood pressure, heart rate, and immune system functioning, and is linked to allergies, snoring, sleep apnea, and jaw and dental problems.

According to Nestor (2020), there are also differences between breathing through the right versus left nostril. Huh? If you skip to the *The How* section below, you can learn about Alternate Nostril Breathing (*nadi shodhana; nadi* means "channel" and *shodhana* means "purification").

- *Right nostril breathing:* The right nostril is our "gas pedal," because breathing through this channel activates the sympathetic nervous system, the fight-or-flight branch of our autonomic nervous system (ANS). To try this, plug your left nostril and take a few breaths through your right nostril. Right nostril breathing puts our bodies in an alert state, indicated by elevated temperature, cortisol levels, blood pressure, and heart rate. Breathing primarily through this right channel also sends more blood to the opposite side of the brain, primarily the left side of our prefrontal cortex (PFC). Research in brain lateralization has demonstrated that the left side of our brains, specifically the left PFC, has stronger associations with logic and decision-making.

- *Left nostril breathing:* In contrast, the left nostril is our "braking system," and has stronger connections with the parasympathetic nervous system, the complementary rest-and-digest branch of the ANS. When this branch is activated, the inverse is observed: a reduction in temperature, cortisol levels, blood pressure, and heart rate, leading to a calming response in our bodies. To try this, plug your right nostril and take a few breaths through your left nostril. This left channel is also more deeply connected to the right side of the brain, primarily the right PFC, and has a stronger association with creativity and emotions.

Ideally, the body functions optimally when in equilibrium, a balance between the more active left side and the more relaxing right side of the brain.

Tip 2: Slow down your breathing.

Slowing down breathing is optimal, as it helps balance oxygen and carbon dioxide levels in the body. But what do we mean by *slow?* What is the optimal pace when it comes to breathing? It turns out that the magic number to highlight is 5.5.

- Inhale for 5.5 seconds.

- Exhale for 5.5 seconds.

- The result is 5.5 breaths (and approximately 5.5 litres of breath) per minute.

Research to support this 5.5-second inhale followed by an exhale of the same duration was first proposed by Stephen Elliott, author of *The New Science of Breath* (Elliot, 2005, as cited in Nestor, n.d.). His technique, referred to as coherent or resonant breathing, was popularized by psychiatrists Richard Brown and Patricia Gerbarg, authors of *The Healing Power of the Breath (2012)*. Research by Bernardi and his colleagues (2001, as cited in Nestor, 2020), also demonstrates the sweet spot of 5.5 in their study that explored this breathing pattern in relation to reciting prayer/mantra. In their study, participants recited a Buddhist mantra as well as the original Latin version of the rosary, the Catholic prayer cycle of the Ave Maria that interestingly reflected this 5.5 breaths-per-minute cycle. They found that breathing in this way led the body to enter a "state of coherence, when the functions of heart, circulation, and nervous system are coordinated to peak efficiency." Research by Lin and her colleagues (2014) further highlights the health benefits of the 5.5 breathing pattern, as they provide evidence that it is related to increases in heart rate variability (HRV), a measure of the variation in time between consecutive heartbeats, reflecting the healthy functioning of the autonomic nervous system. Higher HRV is linked with stronger vagus nerve functioning and with the body's ability to calm down and return to baseline after a stressful event.

Tip 3: Extend your exhalation.

There is evidence that extending one's exhalation has added benefits. Lengthening exhalation engages the parasympathetic nervous system via the vagus nerve. Vagus nerve activity is "suppressed during inhalation and facilitated during exhalation and slow respiration cycles" (Chang et al., as cited in Gerritsen & Band, 2018). See Gerritsen and Band's (2018) comprehensive review paper for an in-depth exploration of how we can intentionally hack our vagus nerve and stimulate a relaxation response by simply breathing slowly and deeply with extended exhalations.

THE HOW

The Calming Breath (slow & deep)

- *Diaphragmatic Breathing:* Many times, when dealing with difficult emotions or situations, we forget to return to the one thing that grounds us in the present moment: our breath. When feeling anxious or overwhelmed, we can deepen our breaths and engage in diaphragmatic breathing. If you feel comfortable, gently put one hand on your heart and the other hand on your belly. Take a deep breath through your nose and feel your chest and belly expand as your hands move away from your spine. With an extended exhale through your nose, feel your hands return to their starting position. Count your breaths in and out. If you feel comfortable, close your eyes or soften your gaze. Remember the magic number, 5.5! If you cannot elongate your breaths to 5–6 second inhales and equal length or, optimally, longer exhales, you can start with a shorter duration such as 3 seconds and work your way up. Also, although 5.5 seconds is often highlighted, it does not matter if we are exact, as long as we attempt to reach this general range with our breaths.

FOCUS BOX: WHAT IS THE VAGUS NERVE?

This set of nerves (one on the left and the other right) are the longest cranial nerves in our bodies. It stems from the medulla in the brainstem, the unconscious and "primitive" part of our brain, and reaches down to the various organs, including the lungs, heart, and the gut. It is this nerve that is highlighted in our discussions of the mind-body connection, specifically the "gut-brain" connection. The vagus nerve is key to our braking system as it calms the body by engaging the parasympathetic nervous system, the "rest-digest" portion of the autonomic nervous system. In *WOW Tip 4: Practice Self-Care*, we will explore how we can stimulate this relaxation response and elevate our vagal tone by engaging in various self-care activities.

FIGURE 6: VAGUS NERVE

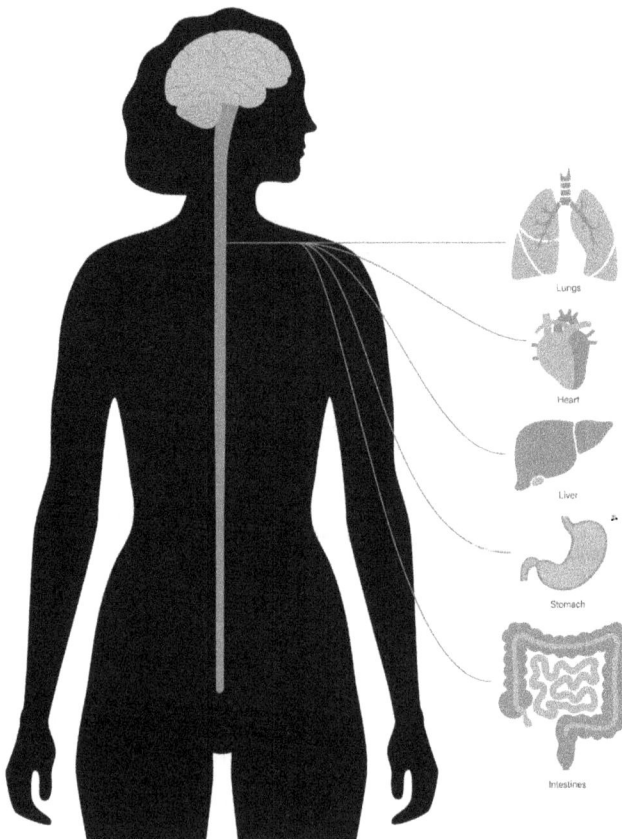

Source: Adobe Stock Photo

- *1 Inhale:2 Exhale—Calming Breath:* Make the length of your exhalation twice as long as your inhalation. This 1:2 ratio calms the body and enables the heart rate to slow down. As highlighted in the previous paragraph, breathe into your belly area.

We should come back to our breath not only when we feel our bodies revving up, but also as a general practice. Set a gentle-sounding alarm on your phone a few times during your day as a reminder to pay attention to your breath. Throughout the day, come back to the breath, the one aspect of you that is always with you and that has the power of being a transformative force in your life.[12]

The Invigorating Breath

- *2 Inhale:1 Exhale—Invigorating Breath:* Make the length of your inhalation twice as long as your exhalation. This 2:1 ratio invigorates the body by providing it with a flood of oxygen; it's great for when you're feeling tired or have low energy.

Other variations

- *Square Breathing:* Take a deep breath in … hold … let it out … hold … and repeat. Envision a square, and that you are moving around the perimeter with each portion. You may keep it simple and use the same length of time for each part (e.g., four seconds each to inhale, hold, exhale, and hold), or you can vary the durations.

- *Alternate Nostril Breathing (nadi shodhana):* According to physician Melissa Young, after taking a seat on a chair or on the floor with a tall, long spine, follow these basic steps (taken verbatim from Cleveland Clinic, 2022):

Step 1. To start, exhale through your mouth, making a "whooshing" sound.

Step 2. Bring your right hand up to your nose, with your index finger hovering

---

[12] Some individuals, many with a history of trauma, do not find paying attention to their breath to be relaxing or comforting. If this is your experience, listen to your body and find something that works for you. It could be grounding into your physical body by feeling your feet contact the floor or your back against the chair. Engage your physical senses as you take in your external environment—what can you see, hear, feel, taste, and smell? You can also bring to mind a kind word or phrase such as "love," "gratitude," "All is well," or "I am enough," or visualize a loved one, a pet, or a special place. Especially if you are in an agitated state, finding an object of focus can ground you into the present moment. Over time, you may find that you have an evolving relationship with your breath. We will discuss this topic in more detail in *WOW Tip 5: Cultivate Mindfulness.*

over your left nostril and your thumb hovering over your right nostril.

Step 3. Use your thumb to block your right nostril. Inhale through your left nostril.

Step 4. Use your index finger to block your left nostril. At this point, both nostrils should be held closed.

Step 5. With both nostrils blocked, hold your breath for a beat or two.

Step 6. Release your thumb to unblock your right nostril and exhale.

Step 7. Take a pause at the bottom of your exhale. Then, keeping your left nostril closed, inhale through your right nostril.

Step 8. Use your thumb to block off your right nostril. With both nostrils held closed, hold your breath again for a beat or two.

Step 9. Release your index finger to unblock your left nostril and exhale.

In summary, take a deep inhale through your left nostril and exhale through the right. Then, take a deep inhale through your right nostril and exhale through the left. Your thumb is used to close the nostril when not inhaling or exhaling.

WOW TIP 2:
SLEEP

THE WHAT

If there is one thing that I know from teaching the subject of sleep for 20+ years, it's that sleep is a priority in terms of healthy habits, and the quantity and quality of one's sleep can be a game changer.

Let us start with a discussion of some sleep basics. There are two major categories of sleep:

1. *NREM (Non-Rapid Eye Movement) sleep:* This category of sleep is further subdivided into substages, ranging from Stage 1 (light sleep) to Stage 4 (deep sleep).[13] This is our "quiet sleep." Our brain, heartbeat, and breathing slow down, and our bodies begin to rest. Our body temperature lowers, and there is little body movement when moving into deeper, restorative sleep. This is when our body recharges and we consolidate our memories. If we do not get enough NREM sleep, we wake up feeling tired and groggy.

2. *REM (Rapid-Eye Movement) sleep:* As the name highlights, there is a lot of movement behind our eyelids. This is in stark contrast to what is observed in the body. Although we refer to REM sleep as being our "active sleep" as our brain during REM sleep looks very similar to our brain during our waking hours, our skeletal muscles, except for our eyes, heart, and lungs, are paralyzed. It is during REM sleep that we dream, and this paralysis protects us from acting out our dreams. If you enter this stage of sleep, you will dream, even if you do not remember your dreams the next morning. This part of sleep is also crucial for creativity and what sleep expert Matthew Walker calls "emotional first aid," when we process the emotional aspect of our lives and REM helps to "take the edge off" these experiences (Walker, 2020b).

Sleep Cycles

When you put your head on your pillow with the intention to fall asleep, you enter Stage 1 sleep. As you fall asleep, you then progress to Stage 2, then 3,

---

[13] In some writings, the deepest level of sleep is sometimes referred to as Stage 3 sleep; reference to Stage 3 sleep as the deepest level is an amalgamation of Stages 3 and 4 in other writings. In this book, I will refer to Stage 4, indicated by the presence of delta waves in the brain, as our deepest level of sleep.

then 4, before eventually moving back to Stage 3, then 2, and then entering the first cycle of REM sleep. This entire sequence lasts approximately 90 minutes. This is repeated a second time, and then the pattern changes, even though the amount of time per cycle remains unchanged. After two cycles, we are less likely to cycle back down to the deeper levels of sleep; instead, we are more likely to cycle between Stage 2 and REM sleep. The amount of time that we spend in REM sleep gets progressively longer with subsequent cycles of sleep. Thus, the ratio of NREM to REM sleep changes throughout the night as we spend most of our time in deep sleep—Stages 3 and 4 in the first half of the night, then switching to increasing amounts of time in Stage 2 and REM for the second half. This is important because if we are not getting enough sleep, such as getting only 6 versus 8 hours of sleep, there may be some consequences of losing more than 50% of REM sleep in those final two "missed" hours.

FIGURE 7: THE SLEEP CYCLE

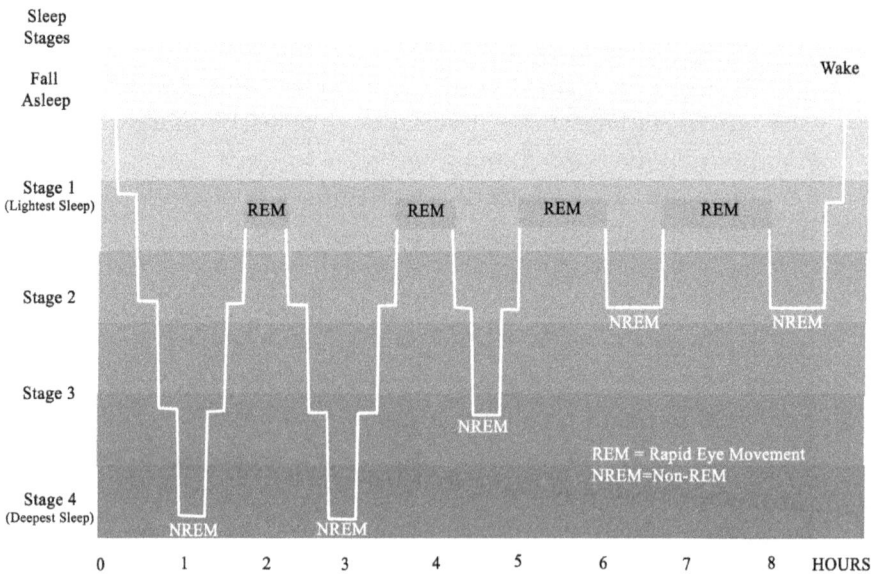

Source: Adobe Stock Photo

THE WHY

> *Every major system, tissue, and organ of your body suffers*
> *when sleep becomes short. No aspect of your health can retreat*
> *at the sign of sleep loss and escape unharmed. Like water from*
> *a burst pipe in your home, the effects of sleep deprivation will*
> *seep into every nook and cranny of biology, down into your cells,*
> *even altering your most fundamental self—your DNA.*

~ Matt Walker

Getting adequate sleep, approximately seven to nine hours for most of us,[14] has been linked to improved performance in all key areas of functioning. In contrast, sleep loss is associated with a shortened lifespan, and has been linked to detrimental consequences, as highlighted in our opening quotation. For example, sleep deprivation can mimic many mental health issues such as anxiety disorders, mood disorders, and ADHD; what *looks like* a psychological disorder may be the consequence of sleep deprivation. Many times, we fail to consider our sleep patterns, both in terms of the quantity and quality of our sleep, when we are distressed or have other symptoms or problems. Sleep issues, such as insomnia, are often conceptualized as symptoms of mental health issues and other ailments. But there are many studies that show that sleep problems can contribute to and/or exacerbate these experiences, within the context of mental health issues or not. Evidence of the connection between sleep and mental health is seen in the growing number of studies that show that better sleep can reduce ADHD-like symptoms in children, reduce anxiety, and improve one's mood. To learn more about the consequences of not getting enough sleep, check out Matthew Walker, author of the book *Why We Sleep* and curator of a series of mini-TED Talks entitled *Sleeping with Science*. In his TED Talk *Sleep Is Your Superpower*, he starts his presentation with this fact: "Men who sleep five hours a night have significantly smaller testicles than those who sleep seven hours or more" (Walker, 2019). You are curious, right? Watch his talk to see what else he has learned in his sleep lab. Table 2 provides a brief summary of some of the research cited in this book.

---

[14] Please note that this recommended range applies to adults aged 18–64. Research demonstrates that sleep duration varies across the lifespan and is influenced by one's genetics, among other factors. Chaput and his colleagues (2018) cite recommendations from various American and Canadian authorities on the subject, including the National Sleep Foundation, American Academy of Sleep Medicine (AASM), Sleep Research Society (SRS), and the Canadian Society for Exercise Physiology (CSEP). For simplicity, according to CSEP (2021), recommendations across the lifespan are as follows: newborns 0–3 months, 14–17 hours; infants 4–11 months, 12–16 hours; toddlers 1–2 years, 11–14 hours; preschoolers 3–4 years, 10–13 hours; children 5–13 years, 9–11 hours; teenagers 14–17 years, 8–10 hours; adults 18–64, 7–9 hours; and older adults, 7–8 hours.

TABLE 2: SOME CONSEQUENCES OF SLEEP DEPRIVATION

PHYSICAL	PSYCHOLOGICAL/ EMOTIONAL	COGNITIVE
Alzheimer's disease Stroke Chronic pain Cancer Diabetes Heart attack Infertility Weight gain Obesity Type 2 diabetes Immune deficiency	Emotional reactivity ["too much emotional gas pedal (amygdala) and not enough regulatory brake (prefrontal cortex)"] Anxiety Depression Bipolar disorder Suicide Substance use (plus increased relapse rates)	Attention deficits (microsleeps— momentary lapses of attention—can be fatal, as seen in an increased risk of car crashes) Memory and learning deficits (for example, refer to "Why are all-nighters bad for you?" on page 46 in this book)

THE HOW

Tips for Better Sleep:

- *Use your bed only for sleep.* Of course, you may be using your bed for other activities, but be mindful of what you are using your bed/bedroom for. For example, if you are writing your papers on your laptop on your bed, preparing a presentation for an upcoming board meeting, or engaging in a stressful activity, your bedroom may not be a place of tranquility.

- *If you can't sleep, get out of bed.* If you have been awake for approximately 25 minutes, leave your room and find something boring to do (Walker, 2020c). Do you have a dull book to read, such as an instruction manual for your coffee maker? Do not pull out your cell phone or device to browse sites, for several reasons, including blue light and engagement. Instead, turn to an activity that will make you sleepy; this is not the time to organize your closet or to clean your baseboards.

- *Establish a consistent, relaxing ritual.* When it comes to raising kids, parents know how important it is to incorporate a bedtime routine.

Do the same for yourself! What will signal to you that sleep is on its way? Maybe a hot shower then reading for 30 minutes (not on a digital device) before heading to bed. These signals and cues can help you set a sleep routine.

- *Set your alarm for the same time each day (7 days/week).* This one can be challenging. You may feel that because you need to be up early during the week, you want to use your weekends to sleep in. Although this may be a great thing to do for those of us who do not have problems with sleep, it is not one to consider early on while establishing a sleep routine. It is important to go to bed *and* to get up at the same time *every* day! Note: Some people believe that sleep is like a bank—if you don't get enough sleep during the week, you can "make up for it" during weekends by accumulating extra hours to "bank" for the upcoming week. Unfortunately, sleep does not work this way. You cannot accumulate sleep debt and then make up for lost time later (Walker, 2020c).

- *Exercise regularly.* Exercise is linked with overall well-being. Research confirms the relationship between exercise and sleep; the more we exercise, the better we sleep. But consider the timing of your exercise. Some professionals advise not to exercise too close to bedtime as it can be stimulating and interfere with getting good sleep. But you know your body best. I know some individuals who are exhausted after a rigorous workout, thus exercising in the evening aids their ability to sleep.

- *Consider your diet.* Establish regular mealtimes, and don't eat heavy or spicy foods before bed.

- *Limit your consumption of caffeine and nicotine.* Both substances interfere with your ability to get good sleep, as they are both classified as stimulants because they increase activity in our central nervous system (CNS). Some rely on caffeine to energize them in the morning. One misconception about caffeine is that it *gives us* energy; instead, caffeine forces us to release the energy we already have stored. If you do drink coffee/tea or consume some other caffeinated substance, refrain from doing so in the hours before bed. According to Walker (2017), caffeine's half-life is 5 to 7 hours. If you drink coffee, half of the caffeine will still be circulating in your system 5 to 7 hours later; one-quarter is still present 5 to 7 hours after that, making it harder for you to get to, and stay, asleep. He also highlights the fact that this substance can change the *quality* of your sleep, specifically the duration of time you spend in deep NREM sleep—Stages 3 and 4, the restorative part of our sleep. That is why you may wake up tired and groggy even if you have been lying in bed for a sufficient time. Nicotine is classified as a stimulant because it activates the CNS and can interfere with sleep, even though for some it "takes the edge off" and "relaxes" them.

- *Limit your alcohol consumption.* Alcohol is a depressant, meaning it decreases the activity in our CNS. From this, you may think that alcohol would be a good sleep aid, but think again! Although consuming increasing amounts of alcohol may help you get to sleep, it may have negative consequences on the quality of your sleep and your ability to stay asleep. In fact, if you look at the brain waves associated with the different stages of sleep, you will observe that the delta waves of deep NREM sleep are often interrupted. Walker (2017) explains that this kind of "sedation" is not equivalent to natural sleep; instead, it is like the brain has been switched off, preventing the normal firing of brain cells, especially in the cortex, the outer layer of the cerebrum. He explains that it may also block REM sleep, the phase of sleep that is imperative for emotional and mental health and creativity.

- *Incorporate relaxation activities, such as mindfulness meditation, into your regimen.* What activities are relaxing to you?

- *Take an inventory of your room.* In a previous tip, I encouraged you to create a relaxing atmosphere in your bedroom by getting those stressful items/activities/cues out of there. Other things to pay attention to are the room's temperature, darkness, and noise level. First, you are more likely to get to and stay asleep in a cool room, ideally 65°F or 18°C (Walker, 2020c). If your room is too hot, put on a fan, open a window if this is a safe option, or turn on an air conditioner. Likewise, you need to ensure that your room is dark, because melatonin is released in darkness. Are the shades on your windows blocking the light from outside? Your best investment may be to purchase blackout shades/blinds. If there is light from under your bedroom door, roll up a towel to block it out. If these options are not available, purchase a sleep mask or consider making one; get creative with a headband or scarf. Finally, minimize the amount of noise you are exposed to. If there are noises that are outside of your control, such as a dog barking or street noise, purchase a white noise machine or invest in some earplugs. To the best of your ability, limit the amount of stimulation coming in through your senses.

- *Limit your use of technology before bed—and perhaps in general.* I am an advocate for changing our relationship with technology, which means setting boundaries. Can you consider turning off your technology for a period of time before bed? If this sounds impossible, can you envision taking some small steps in this direction? Maybe start by shutting off your technology 10 minutes before bed. Consider where you store your technology. Do you keep your phone/device beside your bed? Research shows that the blue light emitted from phones/devices interferes with your sleep, as it impacts melatonin release. But it isn't just this physical component. There is a psychological piece as well: the *association* of your phone with those other stressors in your life. Many times, when I offer the suggestion to keep phones in another room, individuals will often say that their phones are their alarm clock. If you are having problems with sleep, the research suggests you will be better served by investing in a $20 alarm clock and keeping your phone out of your room. For some additional tips on how you can tweak your relationship with your technology, go to *WOW Tip 11: Create a New Relationship with Your Tech Devices.*

Before I leave this section, I will answer some popular questions I am asked when teaching this topic.

Is there a magic number when it comes to sleep?

Not exactly! Although most of us would benefit from getting seven to nine hours of sleep, there are some individual differences when it comes to sleep. Some of us may fall into the category of "short sleepers," where we feel refreshed after getting less than six hours of sleep.[15] On the other end of the continuum, there are "long sleepers"; they generally need more than nine hours of sleep. Most of us will benefit for aiming for approximately eight hours of sleep. So how do you know *your* number? The answer is the way that I respond to many questions I am asked in positive psychology: *Listen to your body!* When it comes to finding your sweet spot, refrain from using an alarm clock to get up. When do you naturally get up in the morning? Experiment

---

[15] Approximately 1% of individuals are natural short sleepers (Schmidt, 2019). A larger percentage of people *believe* they are short sleepers, and that they are performing just fine on less than six hours of sleep. Every time I teach this topic in class, I have many hands raised when I ask if there are any short sleepers in the crowd. If you think you are part of this elite 1% group, you may want to think again; chances are you are simply sleep-deprived and can benefit from an additional one, two, or more hours of sleep!

with this; if you need your alarm clock to wake up in the morning, you are likely not getting enough sleep. Note: Children and teens need *more* sleep, in general. With many youths staying up late at night, there can be some major consequences in all areas of functioning. Keep this in mind when interpreting kids' "difficult" and perhaps "erratic" behaviours. Do they have a mental health or "anger management" issue, or can their behaviours be better understood with this lens of sleep deprivation? Perspective matters!

Are naps good for you?

Are you getting enough sleep? If yes, then a short nap during the day may be beneficial as it can improve your capacity to learn and memorize, and it can positively impact your physiological functioning (e.g., immune system and cardio boosts). But, if you are *not* getting enough sleep, taking a mid-day nap may interfere with getting a good night's sleep. When we wake up in the morning, an endogenous chemical in our brains called adenosine starts to accumulate throughout the day, contributing to "sleep pressure." Taking a nap releases some of this pressure, thus possibly interfering with your nighttime sleep (Walker, 2017).

Why are all-nighters bad for you?

All-nighters are detrimental for multiple reasons, including memory and learning. Walker (2020a) refers to sleep as our "memory weapon." First, we need sleep *before* we learn. He uses a sponge analogy; when we are well-rested, we enter learning situations like a sponge, soaking up everything. Second, we need sleep *after* we learn, because it aids memory consolidation, the part of the process in which we file our learning away into memory.

WOW TIP 3:
EXERCISE

THE WHAT

We need to move our bodies! As a society, we have become the most sedentary that we have ever been in history. Many of our jobs are at desks and in front of computers, and in our leisure time we occupy our time scrolling through our cell phones, watching television, and playing video games. At all ages, many people are not meeting the minimum requirements for movement as set by Canadian exercise guidelines. As a result, we are becoming the unhealthiest we have ever been.

THE WHY

Exercise should be a priority for all of us. It is described as a foundational habit, meaning that once a person starts to exercise, other good habits follow. Individuals who regularly exercise report that they sleep and eat better, compared to individuals who do not. Psychiatrist John Ratey and writer Eric Hagerman wrote a thought-provoking book entitled *Spark* (2008), in which they outline many physical, cognitive, and mental health benefits of exercise. Although the physical benefits of exercise are more commonly known, Ratey and Hagerman demonstrate that exercise can improve our cognitive abilities, including attention, memory, decision-making, and creativity, as well as aid in the treatment of various psychological disorders.

Physical Benefits

Physical activity benefits every system in our bodies, as it is associated with a decreased risk of cardiovascular disease, type 2 diabetes, various cancers, weight gain, and it strengthens our bones. These advantages can be seen when individuals regularly engage in activities that increase their heart rate, coupled with weight-bearing exercises.

Cognitive Benefits

Exercise increases our energy, interest, and motivation to engage in activities that are important to us, while simultaneously shifting the way we view ourselves and our self-concepts so that we start feeling better about ourselves. This is a direct result of the change in important neurotransmitters and hormones in our brain and throughout our bodies, including serotonin, dopamine, norepinephrine, vascular-endothelial growth factor, and brain-derived neurotrophic factor. This last growth hormone has been described by many as a sort of "miracle grow" for our brains; it helps maintain healthy neurons and create new ones, leading to learning benefits. In *Spark*, the authors describe a US high school with a low obesity rate, only 3% compared to the national average of 30%, and highlight their relatively superior academic performance. This is correlational data, but they strengthen their claim that these benefits are the *result* of exercise by reporting studies that show performance on various tasks improves immediately following a short burst of exercise, relative to groups that are tested later in the day. The changes in the brain from exercise appear to positively affect the students' cognitive performance. This has been shown with creativity exercises; a short burst of exercise prior to a brainstorming session can increase individuals' creative outputs. Keep this in mind the next time you are walking into a class, test, or meeting; consider taking a brisk walk before sitting down to learn or complete a task.

Mental Health Benefits

In the sphere of mental health, there is mounting evidence to suggest that exercise is an effective treatment for various mental health issues, including anxiety, depression, and ADHD. Many studies have shown that when exercise is compared to psychotropic medications including selective serotonin reuptake inhibitors (SSRIs), the effectiveness of exercise is often on par with and sometimes greater than these medications, especially in the long term.[16]

THE HOW

How much do we need to move?

Table 3 lists the recommendations outlined by the Canadian Society for Exercise Physiology. To start, calculate your maximum heart rate (HR) by subtracting your age from 220. Then, determine the intensity of your workouts:

- low intensity = 55–65% of maximum HR

- moderate intensity = 65–75% of maximum HR

- high intensity = 75–90% of maximum HR

For example, if you are 40 years old, your maximum HR is 180 (220 minus

---

[16] If you have a prescription for a psychotropic medication, please do not interpret this finding as medical advice to stop taking your prescription. Please consult your doctor and/or healthcare professional for guidance in deciding how to best support your mental health. It could be that a combination of medication and an exercise regimen will be your best course of action. Do not wean yourself off a prescribed medication without medical support and supervision.

40). For a low-intensity workout, your HR will be in the 99–117 HR range. A moderate intensity workout will be in the 117–135 HR range. A high-intensity workout will be in the 135–162 HR range (Centers for Disease Control and Prevention, 2020).

TABLE 3: EXERCISE GUIDELINES

(taken verbatim from Canadian Society for Exercise Physiology, 2021)

INFANTS & YOUNG CHILDREN (AGED 0–4)	INFANTS (LESS THAN 1 YEAR) Being physically active several times in a variety of ways, particularly through interactive floor-based play—more is better. For those not yet mobile, this includes at least 30 minutes of tummy time spread throughout the day while awake. TODDLERS (1–2 YEARS) At least 180 minutes spent in a variety of physical activities at any intensity, including energetic play, spread throughout the day—more is better. PRESCHOOLERS (3–4 YEARS) At least 180 minutes spent in a variety of physical activities spread throughout the day, of which at least 60 minutes is energetic play—more is better.
CHILDREN & TEENS (AGED 5–17)	MODERATE TO VIGOROUS PHYSICAL ACTIVITY An accumulation of at least 60 minutes per day of moderate to vigorous physical activity involving a variety of aerobic activities. Vigorous physical activities, and muscle and bone strengthening activities should each be incorporated at least 3 days per week. LIGHT PHYSICAL ACTIVITY Several hours of a variety of structured and unstructured light physical activities.
ADULTS (AGED 18–64)	MODERATE TO VIGOROUS PHYSICAL ACTIVITY Moderate to vigorous aerobic physical activities such that there is an accumulation of at least 150 minutes per week. Muscle strengthening activities using major muscle groups at least twice a week. LIGHT PHYSICAL ACTIVITY Several hours of light physical activities, including standing.
OLDER ADULTS (AGED 65+)	MODERATE TO VIGOROUS PHYSICAL ACTIVITY Moderate to vigorous aerobic physical activities such that there is an accumulation of at least 150 minutes per week. Muscle strengthening activities using major muscle groups at least twice a week. Physical activities that challenge balance. LIGHT PHYSICAL ACTIVITY Several hours of light physical activities, including standing.

Be creative about ways that you can increase the amount of exercise you do. Park farther away from your building or get off your bus one stop earlier. When cleaning your house, incorporate a lunge as you clean under your tables or bed. You do not need to run a marathon! Getting outside and raising your heart rate with a brisk walk will help you generate the benefits of a more active lifestyle. Better yet, have a friend join you—on a trail in nature! And when you are ready to prepare dinner, do some bicep curls with cans you grab from your pantry. Every little bit counts. To help put some of these actions into motion, see the final section of this book on *Goal Setting and Achieving*.

WOW TIP 4:
PRACTICE SELF-CARE

Self-care is giving the world the best of you,
instead of what's left of you.

~ Katie Reed

THE WHAT

What does self-care look like to you? There are wide-reaching benefits to carving out time in your day/week to take care of yourself. The strategies mentioned in this section, including sleep and exercise, are forms of self-care. What are other ways you can take care of your mind and body? This is an individual exploration; what might be considered "self-care" for one person may be considered a chore for someone else. Ensure you make time for these activities. As we live our busy lives, we may be tempted to skip them because we feel like we don't have enough time or energy, or we feel that engaging in these activities is selfish. My response to these concerns:

- *Not enough time:* When it comes to our well-being, we need to *make* time. If you feel that you don't even have 10 minutes in your day to walk around the block or sit in meditation, then this is evidence that you desperately need to make the time! I challenge my students to look at how much time they are spending on their phones/technology. Are you guilty of mindlessly scrolling? If so, there may be an opportunity here for you to find time you didn't think you had. Ten minutes less of scrolling may mean that you have some time to engage in a short mindful meditation. For additional ideas about how you can change your relationship with technology and find time for self-care, check out *WOW Tip 11: Create a New Relationship with Your Tech Devices*.

- *Not enough energy:* If you are feeling too tired, this is a cue that you need to practice self-care, instead of getting caught in this endless loop (i.e., too tired → do not practice self-care → too tired)! One of the benefits of self-care is that it boosts energy levels, thereby increasing productivity. When feeling sluggish, we are not performing at our best in terms of the quantity and quality of the work we are doing. By taking care of ourselves, we are more likely to get *more* done in the same amount of time.

- *Perception that self-care is selfish:* I often find women raising this concern (not to say that others may not resonate with this one too). Many in caregiving roles may feel that engaging in some of these "frivolous" activities takes us away from our responsibilities. By practicing self-care, we are more likely to have the energy to engage in these selfless actions as we care for our children, parents, and others. For those who work in a caregiving field, it is even more important to practice self-care to prevent burnout. Remember, "self-care is giving the world the best of you, instead of what's left of you."

THE WHY

According to Gayatri Devi, physician and author of *A Calm Brain* (2012), engaging in meditation, savouring a meal, walking a dog, physical touch (e.g., a warm embrace or a massage), sleep and other self-care activities are ways to engage the vagus nerve and elevate vagal tone (Devi, 2012). To dive into this topic further, revisit our discussion of these benefits in *WOW Tip 1: Breathe*. I also encourage you to read Devi's book to learn more about how we can access our brain's built-in relaxation system.

There can be other advantages. Taking a walk or enjoying a tea with a friend can help us experience the connection benefits we highlight in *WOW Tip 14: Foster Connection*. If these activities are done outdoors in greenspace, even better! Research highlights the numerous physical, psychological, and prosocial benefits of being out in nature (Weir, 2020). As cited in Weir (2020), a review of research by Bratman (2019) demonstrated that connecting with nature is linked with boosts in happiness, well-being, positive affect, positive interactions with others, a greater sense of meaning and purpose, and less mental distress. In another study by Mayer and his colleagues (2009, as cited in Weir, 2020), it is suggested that if you cannot get into greenspace you can still reap the benefits of nature by watching videos depicting natural landscapes, although getting outside in these settings leads to a bigger boost. Get into greenspace as often as you can. Consider bringing nature indoors by adding a plant to a shelf, or even a photo of a beautiful landscape to your wall or computer screensaver. Get creative!

By engaging in these activities, you reaffirm to yourself that you are deserving and worthy of this nourishment. By filling your bucket and replenishing your essential energy reserve, you can continue to do amazing things as you pour your energy into pursuits that are meaningful. Savour the time that you give to yourself.

THE HOW

Anything you find relaxing or reenergizing can be part of your self-care regimen. Perhaps you engage in some of these activities daily, such as spending time each morning reading the newspaper, or occasionally, such as a massage. Make yourself a priority and take time for you!

According to Devi (2012), the key is to uni-task. Focus on the task at hand, without distractions. For example, you can eat a delicious meal without scrolling through your Instagram feed.

Some ideas for self-care:

- Do something creative (paint, draw, knit).

- Spend some time with your pet.

- Take a soothing bath.

- Watch a favourite show or movie.

- Grab a tea/coffee and sit in your favourite coffee shop, sit on your front porch, or browse your local bookstore.

- Go for a hike.

- Watch a sunrise or sunset.

- Play an instrument.

- Gaze at the stars. As a suggestion, use a stargazing app on your phone.

- Bake a sweet dessert.

- Read a book in a comfy chair.

- Book a massage or facial or both.

- Do yoga or some gentle stretches.

- Watch a funny video clip.

We can benefit from setting better boundaries for ourselves. Ask yourself if this is how you want to spend your energy. In the words of Paulo Coelho, "When you say 'yes' to others make sure you are not saying 'no' to yourself." It is time to say "yes" to you!

To help you devise your self-care plan, think about the following:

1. *"Within my day" mini self-care breaks:* How can I take better care of myself throughout my day? If you find yourself sitting in front of your computer for work or school, make sure you take regular breaks. As a recommendation, follow the Pomodoro technique, not only for the sake of your attention, which wanes with time, but for the toll it takes on your physical body.

FIGURE 8: THE POMODORO TECHNIQUE

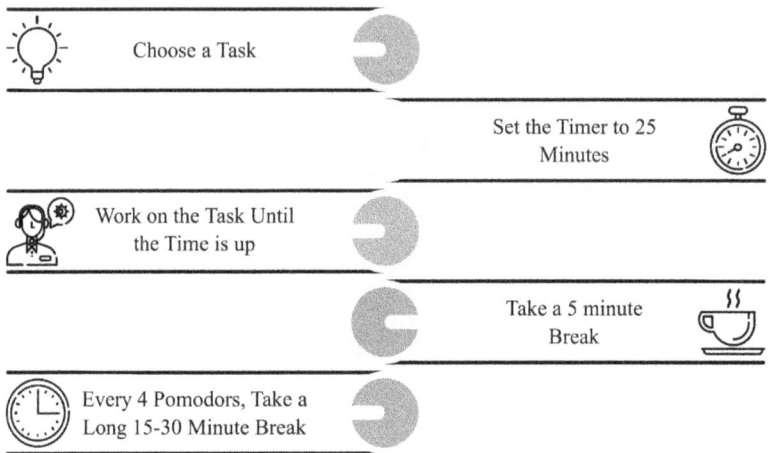

Choose a Task

Set the Timer to 25 Minutes

Work on the Task Until the Time is up

Take a 5 minute Break

Every 4 Pomodors, Take a Long 15-30 Minute Break

Source: Adobe Stock Photo

2. *"Within my week" self-care activities:* These breaks are longer in duration and allow you to relax and/or recharge. Take out your calendar and look at a typical week. Which days will you move (e.g., 30-minute run, 1-hour walk, 1-hour yoga session)? Which days will you relax (by reading a book, journalling, playing a video game, knitting, or taking a bath)? For some of these activities, such as reading the morning paper with coffee or meditating, you may plan to engage in them daily. For others, such as a hike on a trail on the weekend, your goal may be only once per week. To make sure that they happen, get your calendar out and book them in! Can you squeeze in a short mindfulness meditation session as you are waiting for your coffee to brew or brushing your teeth? Attaching a new activity to an established habit will make it more likely to happen (more on this, and other tips, later). You may also want to find an accountability partner. Are you more likely to go out for a 30-minute walk if you have made this commitment with a friend to keep each other accountable? Personally, I can make up any excuse to

avoid an activity when I feel too busy or tired, but I will push through this "hump" if I have committed to doing this activity with a friend. Recently, a group of colleagues at my workplace have created a *sangha* (or "community" in Sanskrit and Pali, among other translations). We are committed to coming together for 10 minutes per day to meditate in silence. I must admit that I finally have a more regular meditation practice since I have found this community. Do you have ideas for what activities you can schedule into your calendar, and how you can make them happen? Although this upfront work of planning may appear to be cumbersome, the research shows that it is an important first step if you want to get from "want to" to "getting it done"!

3. *"Within my year" self-care vacations:* We can all benefit from longer periods to relax/recharge. If you are privileged to work at a job that offers vacation time, ensure you use it! Consider taking a long weekend, or longer, away from any obligations.

Self-Care Plan

Schedule this time in your calendar and stick to it!

THINGS I CAN DO EVERY DAY/ MOST DAYS	THINGS I CAN DO A FEW TIMES PER MONTH	THINGS I CAN DO OCCASIONALLY, 1–2 X PER YEAR
e.g., a 5-minute morning meditation	e.g., a 2-hour hike on the weekend with a friend	e.g., an overnight trip with a friend, a pedicure

WOW TIPS:
MIND

Here are several cognitive strategies that are linked to well-being:

- WOW Tip 5: Cultivate Mindfulness

- WOW Tip 6: Challenge Your Perspective and Mind Chatter

- WOW Tip 7: Make Meaning as You Create Empowering Stories

- WOW Tip 8: Cultivate Gratitude

- WOW Tip 9: Practice Self-Compassion

- WOW Tip 10: Become More Time Affluent

- WOW Tip 11: Create a New Relationship with Your Tech Devices

- WOW Tip 12: Apply Your Strengths

WOW TIP 5:
CULTIVATE MINDFULNESS

Mindfulness is a moment-to-moment, non-judgmental awareness, cultivated by paying attention in a specific way, that is, in the present moment, and as non-reactively, as non-judgmentally, and as openheartedly as possible.

~ Jon Kabat-Zinn

Mindfulness is the energy of being aware and awake to the present moment. It is the continuous practice of touching life deeply in every moment of daily life. To be mindful is to be truly alive, present and at one with those around you and with what you are doing. Through mindfulness, we can learn to live in the present moment instead of in the past and in the future. Dwelling in the present moment is the only way to truly develop peace, both in one's self and in the world.

~ Thích Nhất Hạnh

THE WHAT

Mindfulness can be practiced during a formal meditation, where we may track our breath or tune in to bodily sensations, as well as in less formal settings—when we eat a meal, have a conversation with a friend, or walk to our next class or meeting. Catch yourself from time to time, and ask: "Are my mind and body aligned?" Many times, our minds are somewhere else. A study by Killingsworth and Gilbert (2010) that tracked over 2000 people's real-time reports of their thoughts, feelings, and actions throughout the day found that a whopping 47% of the time their minds were "somewhere else," regardless of the type of activity they were engaging in (the one exception was having sex!). Regardless of whether they were thinking about something negative or neutral, they were *less* happy if they were mind-wandering versus if they were not; no statistical difference was found between mind-wandering about a positive topic versus not mind-wandering. To explore this topic further, watch or listen to Killingsworth's TED Talk entitled *Want to be Happier? Stay in the Moment.*

Reflecting on this research, we would be wise to gently guide our minds back to the present moment throughout our day. Challenge yourself to pay attention to what is happening within your body and surroundings, with curiosity. Mindfulness is about observing and learning to pause in the moment.

Instead of trying to resist or change our experience, can we add a layer of awareness and acceptance without judgment for what is here, right now? That is the essence of *equanimity*.

Mindfulness also recognizes *impermanence*. The essence of this term is that nothing lasts forever. When dealing with challenging emotions, can we be mindful of this and remember that this too shall pass? There is comfort in this realization. On the flip side, good things do not last forever either. When we hold onto the idea that things, either "good" or "bad," last forever, we create a barrier to truly experiencing the here and now—the essence of mindfulness. In addition to our resistance, it is our grasping, clinginess, and attachments that create much of our suffering. In the words of Thích Nhất Hạnh, "It is not impermanence that makes us suffer. What makes us suffer is wanting things to be permanent when they are not."

FOCUS BOX: UNIFIED MINDFULNESS (SHINZEN YOUNG)

During the course of writing this book, I took a sabbatical to learn about mindfulness meditation with Unified Mindfulness. The founder of this system, Shinzen Young, an American mindfulness meditation teacher, studied and incorporated elements of numerous contemplative traditions while formulating this system of mindfulness. To him, mindful awareness consists of two main elements: present-centredness and nonjudgmental attention.

- *Present-centredness:* This is our ability to be aware of what is happening in any given moment, in our bodies and our environments. When we pay attention to the present moment, we can perceive what we are experiencing in our three sensory modalities: see, hear, and feel (Note: feel also includes smell and taste). Within each of these sensory categories, we can have an inner focus—such as See In (mental image), Hear In (mental talk/sound), and Feel In (emotional body sensations)—or an outer focus, consisting of See Out (visual content in the external environment), Hear Out (auditory content in our environment), and Feel Out (physical body sensations, taste, and smell).

- *Nonjudgmental attention:* In Buddhism, there is the parable of the two arrows. When we experience an unfortunate event, the first arrow flies, and it is the one that causes us pain. But suffering is caused when we fire the second arrow—that is, our reactive thoughts and emotions to the first arrow, the grasping or pushing away of the initial pain. In life, we often cannot prevent the first arrow, but we have a choice to fire the second arrow, the unnecessary layer of suffering that we cause. This suffering can take many forms. It can involve stories we create around pain where we remain attached to the hurt—mind chatter consisting of "Here we go again," "There's another example of how I never do anything right," or the many "should" or "should not" stories we construct around our experiences. Or it can involve attempts to suppress or avoid the uncomfortable emotions that accompany the event, such as by drinking, eating, shopping, and scrolling through social media. Instead of grasping or pushing away the experiences that may arise in our bodies, can we have equanimity with them? How do we get to "no second arrow"? According to Shinzen Young, we have options. The first is to *anchor away* from these naturally occurring judgments and reactions until this habit weakens over time, by letting the judging play out in the background while we anchor on another object of focus. The second option would be to *turn toward* the judgment or reaction, and to untangle its components, which include mental image, mental talk, and emotional bodily sensations. Breaking our experience down into smaller, manageable components will allow it to dissolve as we bring equanimity to this disentangling process. Each of these approaches will involve strengthening our attentional skills of concentration, sensory clarity, and equanimity (CCE).

CONCENTRATION	Ability to focus on what is relevant at a given time
SENSORY CLARITY	Ability to track and explore what you're experiencing
EQUANIMITY	Ability to allow sensory experience to come and go without push or pull

To be present-centred and apply nonjudgmental awareness to our experience, these three attentional skills—concentration, sensory clarity, and equanimity—need to be working together:

1. Concentration

Can we focus on what we deem relevant, even briefly? At any moment, we can pay attention to an infinite number of stimuli/sensations within our bodies or in our external environments. Can we choose one object of focus and selectively attend to it, such as the rising and falling of our breath?

2. Sensory Clarity

- *Discrimination (Discernment):* Can we break down our present experience, such as a challenging emotion, into smaller components? What part of this emotion is in my head/body? When looking at what is happening in my "mind," what part of this is mental image (See In), mental talk (Hear In), and emotional bodily sensations (Feel In)? Our ability to be with our emotions is directly related to our ability to untangle our experience. We can become overwhelmed when these components become "coagulated" and stuck; we feel like we are dealing with a large, static mass. Our ability to move from overwhelm to control rests on our ability to "peel back the layers" of our experience (I attribute this "peeling back" phrase to my friend and colleague Tuls).

- *Detection (Sensitivity):* We can only untangle what we can detect! Sometimes what is happening within us, whether it is mental image, mental talk, or an emotional bodily sensation, may be below our conscious awareness. But with time, and as we begin to strengthen our attentional skills, particularly sensory clarity in this case, can what was once undetectable be detected? And as Shinzen Young says, "What is trackable is tractable."

Both discrimination and detection are needed to avoid the emotional hijacking, the overwhelm, that can sometimes follow an unfortunate event.

3. Equanimity

In contrast to the way we often respond to uncomfortable emotions—the "push and pull" of an emotional experience—can we find balance? Not trying to suppress the emotional experience, or identifying/grasping onto it, but instead, just letting it be. As an observer to our experience, can we acknowledge the rising and falling sensations, the impermanent quality to all our experiences, both internal and external? Our experiences are not static/unchanging; if we are curious to track what may be happening in our inner landscape, with reference to physical or emotional pain, can we observe any shifts or subtle changes with time? For example, does a sensation become more or less intense with time? Does it spread? Can you observe the edges/contours of where an emotion may be bubbling up in your body? I have always found it comforting to come back to the phrase "this too shall pass," but with learning this Unified Mindfulness system and the concept of flow, I have found relief in tracking this impermanence in real time. This too *is* passing. When working with tension/discomfort, we can intentionally create equanimity when we maintain a relaxed state as an uncomfortable sensation washes through our bodies. We can create equanimity in our minds by letting go or not attaching to reactive judgments that may arise, and instead bringing some self-compassion to this challenging space.

This above synopsis is extremely brief, and key details were simplified or omitted for brevity purposes. Please visit the *The How* section of this chapter for instructions on how to practice the See-Hear-Feel (SHF) technique. If you are interested in learning more about Unified Mindfulness, I highly recommend the following resources:

1. *Core Training Program (free online program):*
   https://unifiedmindfulness.com/learn-um/

2. *What Is Mindfulness?:*
   https://www.shinzen.org/wp- content/uploads/2016/08/WhatIsMindfulness_SY_Public_ver1.5.pdf

3. *5 Ways to Know Thyself:*
   https://unifiedmindfulness.com/wp- content/uploads/2016/02/Five-Ways-to-Know-Yourself.pdf

THE WHY

Here, we highlight the benefits of engaging in a regular and more formal mindfulness meditation practice,[17] that may include sitting or lying down comfortably, or walking, for a set time. Much of this research has examined the effects of formalized mindfulness-based programs such as Jon Kabat-Zinn's eight-week Mindfulness-Based Stress Reduction (MBSR) program on conditions ranging from those related to mental health, including anxiety and depression, to physical ailments including chronic pain and heart, skin, and immune system issues. There is an accumulating body of research to support the many physical, cognitive, and emotional/mental health benefits associated with a formal practice, including but not limited to reduced rumination, stress reduction, boosts to working memory, increased focus, less emotional reactivity, more cognitive flexibility, and improved relationship satisfaction (Davis & Hayes, 2012). Although this area of research is in its infancy stage, it appears that some of these benefits may reflect underlying physiological changes in the brain and body that occur with consistent, formal practice. To take a deeper dive into the broader physical, cognitive, and emotional benefits of meditation, check out these *Mindful* magazine articles: "The Science of Mindfulness" (https://www.mindful.org/the-science-of-mindfulness) and "Meditators Under the Microscope" (https://www.mindful.org/meditators-under-the-microscope).

There is an abundance of evidence demonstrating that a formal meditation practice can help reduce anxiety and depressive symptoms. For example, mindfulness has been embedded in many mainstream psychotherapies—including Kabat-Zinn's MBSR program; Linehan's Dialectical and Behaviour therapy (DBT); Segal, Teasdale, and Williams's Mindfulness-Based Cognitive

---

[17] Caveat: Please note that many but not all people will experience benefits from a formal meditation practice. In fact, as cited by Foster (2016), mindfulness meditation can have negative effects for some people, especially if they are engaging in an immersive mindfulness practice such as a retreat. But sometimes a negative reaction has been observed when engaging in this practice for as little as 20 minutes per day. Certain psychological disorders including PTSD and/or a history of trauma can increase the likelihood of this type of outcome. Having said that, the psychological, cognitive, and physical benefits of a regular mindfulness practice have been widely demonstrated, and the potential for adverse effects is relatively rare. If you are interested in this topic, I would highly recommend that you read David Treleaven's book *Trauma-Sensitive Mindfulness*, or watch/listen to his free one-hour webinar on the topic (https://davidtreleaven.com/the-truth-about-mindfulness-and-trauma/). In these resources, he highlights some of the potential effects of a mindfulness meditation practice—including flashbacks, heightened emotional arousal, and dissociation—in some individuals with a history of trauma. You may also consider exploring Willouby Britton and Jared Lindahl's The Varieties of Contemplative Experience research project; you will find amazing resources listed on this page: https://sites.brown.edu/britton/research/the-varieties-of-contemplative-experience/.

Therapy (MBCT); and Hayes's Acceptance and Commitment Therapy (ACT)—and its effectiveness across a broad spectrum of mental health issues and symptomatology has been noted in the clinical literature. One issue targeted with these treatments is emotion dysregulation. With mindfulness training, one learns how to skillfully navigate challenging emotions by becoming less reactive to them; one strategy that can help is to untangle our mind chatter from this *feel* experience. Delehanty (2017) describes how meditation blocks the brain's "default mode network," a neural network that is activated when we are "doing nothing"; during these times, we tend to weave together our thoughts and feelings into our self-referential stories. Meditation allows us to notice when our mind wanders and helps to guide our attention back to the present moment. By doing so repeatedly, we become "far less attached to the ongoing narrative we make up about ourselves," Delehanty argues. Some researchers hypothesize that as we practice this skill on a regular basis, we strengthen the connection between the prefrontal cortex (PFC), the "rational" part of the brain that manages this emotional reactivity, and the amygdala, the "emotional" part that triggers this reactivity via the fight-or-flight response. With meditation, it is not that we are ridding ourselves of our narratives, but we are changing our relationship with them. Delehanty cites renowned meditation researchers and long-time practitioners Daniel Goleman, author of *Emotional Intelligence* and *Focus*, and Richard Davidson, author of *The Emotional Life of Your Brain*, and co-authors of *Altered Traits*, as saying that it is "the relationship to the self (that) changes and is not so 'sticky' anymore. The same sorts of thoughts can arise in your mind … but they are lighter: not so compelling, with less emotional oomph, and so float away more easily" (Goleman & Davidson, 2018, as cited in Delehanty, 2017). This is the essence of equanimity. In a demonstration of superior emotion regulation skills, Mingyur Rinpoche, a Tibetan teacher and master, and other long-time meditation practitioners were exposed to a painful blast of heat for 10 seconds, preceded by a 10-second warning. As compared to a control group of novice meditators whose brains were activated immediately after the warning signal was sounded, the expert meditators did not show any reaction to the warning, but exhibited a more intense response to the heat. They also recovered more quickly when this painful event ended. According to Goleman and Davidson (2018, as cited in Delehanty, 2017), "this inverted-V pattern, with little reaction during anticipation of a painful event, followed by a surge of intensity at the actual moment, then swift recovery from it, can be highly adaptive … This lets us be fully responsive to a challenge as it happens, without letting our emotional reactions interfere before or afterward, when they are no longer useful." In their book *Altered Traits* (2018), Goleman and

Davidson describe a study where expert meditators' brains were scanned while viewing troubling images of people suffering (e.g., burn victims). These scans showed that their amygdalae were less reactive, and their brains had stronger connectivity between the PFC and the amygdala. Together, these observations showed that their extensive meditation experience made them "more immune to emotional hijacking."

One final note of caution: If you decide to sift through the evidence purporting the benefits of meditation, be wary of studies that may have problems with research design. Common problems include a lack of a control group, self-selection bias, confounding variables and/or measurement issues, such as the tools used to estimate brain volume. For example, research shows key differences in the brains between expert meditators and novices. It may be tempting to conclude that a meditation practice leads to these types of structural and/or functional changes in the brain. But given that this research is often correlational by design, one cannot be 100% confident about the direction of this cause-effect relationship. It is the hope that future research will involve more rigorous research design, and that longitudinal studies will become more common so that we can track physiological and behavioural changes over time. Ultimately, the aim is to be better able to answer some basic questions about this growing field, such as the effect of duration of practice (e.g., length of daily practice, retreat practice). According to Davidson (as cited in Delehanty, 2017):

> Right now we have absolutely no idea what the optimal strategy for producing enduring change is … These are critical questions that can be addressed scientifically and need to be if this work is really going to have broad impact … We've shown in the laboratory that meditating for a half hour a day for two weeks is enough to produce changes in the brain … Most people recognize that if you go to the gym for two weeks and work out every day with a personal trainer, you'll feel a difference. But those changes aren't going to persist unless you keep exercising. Meditation is very similar. It's a form of mental exercise. And once you begin to experience beneficial changes, it will inspire you to continue practicing for the rest of your life.

A little motivation to start a regular, consistent meditation practice!

THE HOW

When many of us think about mindfulness meditation, we often picture someone practicing in stillness. But we can practice meditation anytime, anywhere. Carving out time in your day to pour your attention into the practice can be done in a variety of ways, and for varying periods of time. Personalize your mindfulness practice to make it your own.

Practicing in Stillness

Can we find some time in our day to sit or lie down to practice? The foundational technique in Unified Mindfulness is called See-Hear-Feel (SHF). In each of these three sensory categories, we can focus *in* by paying attention to mental image (See In), mental talk/sound (Hear In), or emotional bodily sensations (Feel In), or focus *out* by directing our attention to objects in the external environment (See Out), external sound (Hear Out), and physical bodily sensations (Feel Out). As we come into our SHF practice, we can allow our attention to float and land where it may, or we can direct our focus in a particular way, such as only focusing on Feel Out, and tracking the movement of our breath. But when our attention lands, we pour our attention into the experience as we strengthen our concentration and sensory clarity skills. Can we explore what we are seeing, hearing, or feeling? Can we become curious as to what is happening in this space, how it possibly changes as we track our experience? And if during our practice we bump up against an uncomfortable sensation—or in contrast, it is especially pleasurable and we are inclined to grasp and hold on to it—can we bring equanimity to our experience by not pushing and pulling, but *letting it be?*

Here are the suggested steps (please customize your practice):

Step 1. Set your intention; either:

- Allow your attention to float.

- Direct your attention in a particular way. You may choose to explore one or more of the six areas of focus: See In, See Out, Hear In, Hear Out, Feel In, Feel Out. For example, you can focus your attention on the physical sensations in your body (Feel Out), or narrow your focus range within this Feel Out space by directing your attention to your breath only.

Step 2. Note. Once you notice something to focus on, allow your attention to land.

Step 3. Use a label (see, hear, or feel), either out loud or in your mind. This is an optional step, but one that supports our noting practice, especially if we are challenged with distractibility.

Some things to keep in mind:

- If you are becoming overwhelmed, slow down. Remember, you don't have to note and label all experiences.

- If two or more categories apply—for example, you see and hear a car as it drives by—just pick one.

- If you are not noticing much (i.e., a blank screen for see, a quiet mind for hear, or emotional peace for feel), just use the appropriate label and enjoy this rest.

Step 4. Stay for a few seconds and explore the sensation. Get curious! Then repeat, finding the same or new object of focus.

FIGURE 9: SUMMARY OF STEPS

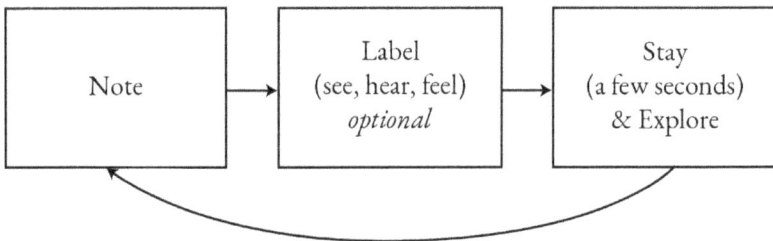

Practicing in Motion

We can apply the SHF technique in each of these instances:

Mindful Eating: The next time you eat a meal, away from your devices and other distractions, slow down and take it in with all your senses—see, hear, and feel. Notice the colour(s), the presentation, the aroma, the texture in your mouth. Really *taste* your food. By slowing down, do you experience this meal in a new way? Do you enjoy it more? Can you add in a layer of mindfulness as you consider how this food arrived on your plate? From the people who picked the food, harvested it, and packaged it, to those who drove it to the grocery store and sold it to you? Can you appreciate the time that went into preparing the food? Can you express gratitude? Considering all these details, can you have a different experience as compared to times when you are consuming technology and mindlessly eating your food?

Morning Routine: The next time you take a shower, can you be more mindful of the experience? Instead of thinking about all the things you will have to do that day, can you feel the water fall on your body? Can you smell the soap or shampoo, and feel the texture of these products on your skin and hair? Can you bring this same awareness to brushing your teeth?

Mindful Walking: As you hike on a trail, embrace your surroundings and activate all your senses! What do you see in front of you … the trees, the animals, and birds? What do you hear … the sound of birds chirping, animals trekking by, or trickling water? Do you feel the sun or breeze on your skin? As you take your next step, feel your heel, arch, ball, then toes touch the earth. If possible, slow down your pace and pay attention to your movement. Savour this experience, and soak in this see-hear-feel space.

Catch yourself in any moment. Pay attention to the full experience, and express pure gratitude for it. Try to "sprinkle your day" with moments of mindfulness, even if only for a few seconds at a time. In Unified Mindfulness, these brief moments—ranging from a few seconds to less than 10 minutes of practice—are called "microhits." Brushing your teeth, waiting for your coffee to drip, or waiting in line at the grocery store now become opportunities to practice. Regardless of what brings us to our practice—a pocket of time in our schedule, or maybe it is out of necessity because we are working with some challenging emotions or about to engage in a difficult conversation—every moment we drop into a mindful space is an opportunity to strengthen our three attentional skills: concentration, sensory clarity, and equanimity (CCE). By finding opportunities throughout our day and making time to engage in a formal practice for as little as 10 minutes, we can elevate our baseline of CCE so that we can better navigate the challenging times in our lives. At these times, pay attention to how this experience shows up in your body. Can you allow yourself to just sit in this space? Can you be curious and make a different choice in the future? Can we learn to *get comfortable being uncomfortable?* With an equanimous heart, we can transform our experience and sense the impermanence, even if only slightly, of these sensations.

One final note for reflection: "If you listen to your body when it whispers, you won't have to hear it scream" (unknown author). Many of us can benefit from becoming more attuned to our bodies, a consequence of strengthening our sensory clarity skills. Many times, our bodies are trying to keep us safe and warn us of a possible, impending danger. Some of us have stories of trauma that are held in our bodies. In Tara Brach's book *Radical Compassion* (2020a), she refers to the concept of our "issues being in our tissues." See *WOW Tip 9:*

Practice Self-Compassion to learn some techniques for beginning this process of healing. There is great wisdom in our bodies, and our body will communicate to us what it needs, if we listen. The many strategies throughout this book can help us regulate many of our uncomfortable emotions and sensations. If we are starting to become agitated/uncomfortable, it will be much easier to intervene—to breathe, to use soothing self-statements, and to practice self-compassion—in the *whispers* rather than the *screams,* the all-encompassing emotions such as full-blown panic or rage. By elevating our baseline of CCE, we can better tune in to this inner wisdom.

Focus Box: "Two monks and a woman" Parable

(as cited in Farmer Sean, 2018)

A senior monk and a junior monk were travelling together. At one point, they came to a river with a strong current. As the monks were preparing to cross the river, they saw a very young and beautiful woman also attempting to cross. The young woman asked if they could help her cross to the other side.

The two monks glanced at one another, because they had taken vows not to touch a woman. Then, without a word, the older monk picked up the woman, carried her across the river, placed her gently on the other side, and carried on with his journey. The younger monk couldn't believe what had just happened. After rejoining his companion, he was speechless, and an hour passed without a word between them. Two more hours passed, then three; finally the younger monk could not contain himself any longer, and blurted out, "As monks, we are not permitted to touch a woman. How could you then carry that woman on your shoulders?" The older monk looked at him and replied, "Brother, I set her down on the other side of the river. Why are you still carrying her?"

What are you holding on to? It is often not the events that happen to us that cause our distress, but our *attachment* to these events and corresponding emotions. Is there an opportunity to *let it go* or to *let it be,* to have a different relationship to the things we have experienced in our life? In neuroscientist Jill Bolte Taylor's book *The Stroke of Insight*, she explains the 90-second rule when it comes to our emotions. "When a person has a reaction to something in their environment," she says, "there's a 90-second chemical process that happens in the body; after that, any remaining emotional response is just the person choosing to stay in that emotional loop" (Bolte Taylor, 2009). It is our attachments, the story we tell ourselves, that prolong this emotional response. We are *firing the second arrow*. Instead, apply mindfulness and use breath or another grounding exercise to ride the waves of the emotion. In the words of Jon Kabat-Zinn, "You can't stop the waves, but you can learn to surf."

WOW TIP 6:
CHALLENGE YOUR PERSPECTIVE
AND MIND CHATTER

The happiness of your life depends
upon the quality of your thoughts.

~ Marcus Aurelius

Source: Adobe Stock Photo

THE WHAT

Part A: Challenging Your Perspective

Please begin by watching this video; in YouTube, search "selective attention test" and view the 1-minute-and-22-second clip posted by Daniel Simons (2010), a psychologist and one of the authors of the study. We will come back to this study shortly.

At any one time, we have access—via our eyes, ears, skin, taste buds, and olfactory receptors—to only a small fraction of the stimuli that are available around us, not only because our attention is limited, but because we simply cannot detect those stimuli that fall below our sensory thresholds. A multitude of species can sense stimuli of which we are completely unaware. But even when we can detect what exists around us as we see, hear, feel, taste, and smell these stimuli, we may not be aware of all of them if we are not paying attention. If we cannot attend to everything in front of us, what are we choosing to pay attention to, on a conscious level or not? At the opening of this section, you viewed a drawing inspired by the *The Blind Men and the Elephant* poem by John Godfrey Saxe. Is it possible that we could all be looking at the same thing, in this case an elephant, but concentrating on a different aspect of it? Can each of these different vantage points be accurate? No one perspective is more accurate than the other. Can we benefit from taking a sidestep and seeing what is in front of us from a different perspective or, better yet, by taking a few steps back and viewing it with a more holistic lens, seeing the elephant rather than focusing on the smaller elements of it? Context is everything!

And now back to that video that you watched. If you kept reading and did not watch the video, please read the footnote at the bottom of this page for a brief description before reading on.[18] In an interesting set of experiments on *inattentional blindness*, individuals are often not aware of a surprising and unexpected event when paying attention to something else, even when this event falls directly in their field of vision (confirmed by eye-gazing trackers). So not seeing the gorilla is not the result of one's eyes not "seeing" it, but that one's mind or attention did not capture it. Is it possible that something has just happened right in front of your eyes or ears and you are not even aware of it? There are other shocking examples in *change blindness* as well. Imagine speaking to someone when right in front of your eyes the person is replaced. In one example, a person ducks down behind a counter and another person pops up. Most of the time, participants do not notice the change, even when the second person looks nothing like the original person! I have seen demonstrations where the two individuals are of other-appearing genders (male-appearing versus female-appearing individuals), in different clothing, and with different voices. Keep this in mind the next time you accuse someone of missing something that appears to be utterly obvious to you.

Perception is another important process that needs to be highlighted. We can all be *seeing* the same situation, but we could be attending to and *interpreting* it in different ways, and our past experiences and learning histories

---

[18] At the start of this video, the words on screen instruct the viewer to "Count how many times the players wearing white pass the basketball." Then we see two teams of three players. The "white" team is in white shirts and blue jeans and the "black" team is wearing all black. For a few seconds, you see each team passing a basketball to members of their own team; two balls are in play. At the end of the first segment, viewers are asked, "How many passes did you count?" Then, after a brief pause, "The correct answer is 15" appears on screen—and then, "But did you see the gorilla?". At this point, the video is rewound, and viewers clearly observe someone in a black gorilla suit walking across the screen, beating his chest briefly when at the centre of the play, then walking off-screen.

influence this process. For example, is the person you are speaking to "lazy," "incompetent," and/or "intentionally causing harm" (dispositional inference), or could this person be doing the best they can in challenging circumstances, perhaps coping with a personal or relational situation of which you are not aware (situational inference)? What are you paying attention to? How are you interpreting ambiguous aspects of the situation (which you are doing—you are just often not aware of it)? How you resolve this ambiguity and ultimately interpret your situation affects how you feel about and respond to it. Consider how many of your disagreements with a friend, family member, colleague, or stranger may in fact be the result of a difference in interpretation, and possibly attention as well.

Part B: Challenging Your Mind Chatter

We suffer more often in imagination than in reality.

~ Seneca

You have power over your mind — not outside events.
Realize this, and you will find strength.

~ Marcus Aurelius

WRITE DOWN SOME OF YOUR NEGATIVE MIND CHATTER

Pay attention to the conversation you have with yourself. Sometimes we say things to ourselves that we would never say to another person! We get stuck in feeling *not good enough* in some way. We may feel that we are deficient in some respect, "not normal," or not worthy of the good things in our lives. At other times, our minds are too past-oriented, and we find ourselves ruminating about the *should-* and/or *shouldn't-haves* (tip: Don't *should* on yourself!). Instead of clinging to the past or grasping for what could have been, is there an opportunity to let something go or let it be? Sometimes our minds are caught in future thoughts, the realm of the *what-ifs*. Often, we worry about things that *may* happen, but that may never actually come to fruition. This is not to say that we should avoid thinking back and reminiscing about the past—perhaps seeing an opportunity for growth if we have dealt with a challenging situation—or that thinking about and planning for the future is not a useful pursuit as we set and work toward achieving our goals. The problem is getting stuck in thoughts that may not serve us.

When we find ourselves getting caught in our thoughts, can we challenge them in some way?

Two thoughts that often get us into trouble are:

1. *Everyone should like me.* Realistically, not everyone will like you, and that's okay! If you are living your true, authentic self, there will be people who will not like you. I love this quote from Rebecca Campbell: "The world is full of people who, no matter what you do, will point-blank not like you. But it is also filled with people who will love you fiercely. *You are not for everyone, and that's ok.*" At the end of the day, you need to come to terms with what you can and cannot control—and what someone thinks about you is definitely something you cannot control. Also, think about it: Do you like everyone you meet? Of course, you don't! Why would you expect anything different of others?

2. *It is awful to fail/make mistakes; I am perfect.* In reality, we are human—we will make mistakes and experience failure. What matters is what you do with it. Are you going to use it as a learning opportunity (growth mindset)? Ask yourself: "What can I learn to do differently next time?" Find comfort in the words of Nelson Mandela the next time you experience failure or a disappointment: "I never lose. I either win or learn."

When dealing with a perceived failure or setback, remember what success looks like most of the time. It is not a straight line upward; sometimes we take a side-step or two steps backward before moving forward.

FIGURE 10: WHAT SUCCESS ACTUALLY LOOKS LIKE

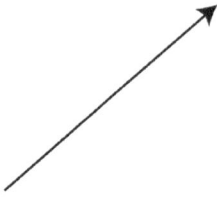

What people *think*
success looks like

What success
actually looks like

Source: Adapted from Martin (2012)

Remind yourself that success often happens by taking risks. It is about *getting comfortable being uncomfortable*. Putting yourself out there without knowing how you will be received takes vulnerability and courage. Many times, failure is what propels us to make progress. Look at the greats. Many athletes, inventors, writers, actors, and creative minds took risks and failed *many* times (check out the *Famous Failures* video on YouTube). Failure is part of success. Consider the iceberg illustration on the next page. Under the surface of those success stories are many failures and disappointments. Like Thomas Edison said, "I have not failed. I've just found 10,000 ways that won't work." Can you see your life's path as a series of "experiments," not failures? Your lightbulb may be just around the corner!

And when you hurt someone, even if unintentionally, with your words or actions/inactions, seek solace and compassion in these quotes:

Sometimes good people make bad choices.
It doesn't mean they are bad people. It means they're human.

~ Sui Ishida

You are imperfect, you are wired for struggle,
but you are worthy of love and belonging.

~ Brené Brown

FIGURE 11: THE ICEBERG ILLUSION

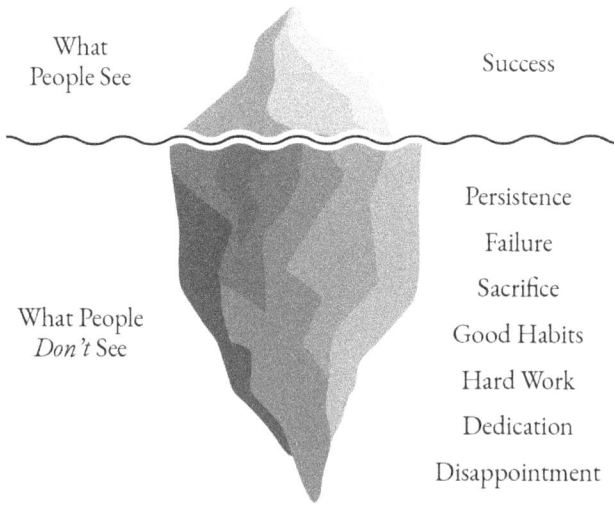

What
People See

Success

What People
Don't See

Persistence

Failure

Sacrifice

Good Habits

Hard Work

Dedication

Disappointment

Source: Adapted from Duckworth (2019)

As human beings, we will make mistakes—lots of them. Instead of beating yourself up, consider the opportunity you may have in making amends, and/or use this opportunity to do better in the future. Can you acknowledge your wrongdoing and apologize? In the words of Maya Angelou, "Do the best you can until you know better. Then when you know better, do better."

Challenge yourself to develop a more optimistic explanatory style when unfortunate things happen. Martin Seligman (2006) encourages us to explain these events as *not* personal but situational, *not* pervasive but objective, and *not* permanent but temporary, as a more optimistic frame is associated with better overall health and well-being outcomes. In contrast, a pessimistic explanatory style makes sense of these same occurrences in a very different way: personal ("It's all me!"), pervasive ("Nothing ever goes right!"), and permanent ("This will never change!"). Are these statements really true? Like a detective, gather the evidence. Let us challenge each one in further detail:

- *Personal ("It's all me!"):* Can you take 100% responsibility for this unfortunate event? Are there no other person(s) or situational factors that share some responsibility?

- *Pervasive ("Nothing ever goes right!"):* Is it true that nothing has *ever* gone right for you? Or are you concentrating on the negatives when scanning your past? When in a negative mindset and experiencing challenging emotions, we tend to narrow our focus. Is it possible that you are concentrating on other "failures" without acknowledging other possible wins or at least "non-failures"?

- *Permanent ("This will never change!"):* Will things *never* get better? Can we reflect on factors within our control that can help improve our situation in the future—for example, our effort and practice? How I allocate my time is something that I *can* control. If I choose to study more or differently or with a study group, could these changes lead to a different result?

Be a critical thinker! Whenever we use "always" or "never" in our thoughts, they are rarely true.

I will leave you with some questions to ask yourself when you are struggling with some difficult thoughts/emotions:

- *If my best friend thought this, what would I say to them?* When a friend struggles after a disappointment—a failing grade or a gut-wrenching breakup—we are often a soft place to land. We are not questioning whether they will ever be successful in their academic program or career, or whether they will ever find someone else that will ever love them. Instead, we approach them with gentleness and compassion. We help our friend see their situation from a clearer perspective. Say these compassionate things to yourself!

- *Are you sure?* Come back to the question offered by Thích Nhất Hạnh (1999), posed in the introduction of this book. Is there another way to see and interpret this situation? Is it really catastrophic, even if it feels that way? Just because it feels that way doesn't mean it is. That is the essence of *emotional reasoning*, one of the cognitive distortions highlighted by Aaron Beck, psychiatrist and founder of Cognitive Therapy, later broadened to Cognitive Behavioural Therapy (CBT). Is there an opportunity in this situation? In her book *Mindset*, psychologist Carol Dweck (2007) recommends that we approach challenging situations with a growth mindset. Ask yourself if there is something you can learn from this situation. Can you do something differently in the future? And upon reflection, you may realize that what is in front of you is not so bad after all. Or, you may look at your situation and realize that it absolutely does suck! What happened was unfortunate, unfair, or unjust! And this is okay too. If this latter

Focus Box: "A Chinese farmer" Parable

(as cited in McCall, 2018)

Once upon a time there was an old farmer who had worked his crops for many years. One day his horse ran away. Upon hearing the news, his neighbours came to visit. "Such bad luck," they said sympathetically. "Maybe," the farmer replied.

The next morning the horse returned, bringing with it three other wild horses. "How wonderful," the neighbours exclaimed. "Maybe," replied the old man.

The following day, his son tried to ride one of the untamed horses, was thrown, and broke his leg. The neighbours again came to offer their sympathy on his misfortune. "Maybe," answered the farmer.

The day after, military officials came to the village to draft young men into the army. Seeing that the son's leg was broken, they passed him by. The neighbours congratulated the farmer on how well things had turned out. "Maybe," said the farmer.

This story is a good reminder to come back to this point about non-judgmental awareness. We often add a layer of judgment, categorizing and labelling our experiences as either good/bad or right/wrong without considering the possibility that this may not be so. We fall prey to distorted ways of thinking. In this story, the cognitive distortion that is highlighted is *fortune telling*. Is it possible that you are wrong, and the consequence(s) of your situation will not actually play out the way you predict? When confronted with a challenging situation, remember this story and say to yourself, "Maybe … or maybe not" as we return to Thích Nhất Hạnh's (1999) offering of "Are you sure?"

interpretation of events is where you land, can you zoom out of your situation and give yourself some much-needed space? In the grand scheme of life, does this really matter? A visualization that I find helpful is to shift my atmospheric perspective—I zoom out so that my "problem" or challenge is a speck in the grand universe. As an alternative, shift your temporal perspective by picturing yourself in your later years in your rocking chair; will this situation matter at this later stage of life? Most of the time, a difficult situation does not feel the same way even a few days, weeks, or months from now. One recommendation is to watch or listen to Sam Harris's three-minute meditation on gratitude on YouTube. It can help you shift your current perspective on a challenging situation.

- *Are you ruminating or worrying about something that you cannot control?* Epictetus reminds us that "there is only one way to happiness and that is to cease worrying about things which are beyond the power of our will." You will experience many disappointments, failures, challenges, and tragedies in your life. Human struggle is universal. But what is important is how we can move forward not just despite it, but *because* of it. What do we control in our situations? Although there are many things that we cannot control or influence, there are some things that we can—primarily, our thinking and ability to challenge our perspective.

If you are struggling with a relational conflict, something that involves at least one other person, consider how these interactions with others are impacting you. What do you control in these situations and future ones? When it comes to other people, you cannot control their thinking or behaviour. But you *can* choose to limit your interactions with others that cause you harm. If this is not possible, you can become more mindful of these interactions and create space for yourself. Additionally, can you approach this person with an open heart and mind? Perhaps this person does not intentionally mean to hurt you. I am not trying to excuse their behaviour or imply that what they are doing is okay, but this acknowledgement can lessen the hurt for you. Or perhaps you can step away from this situation and see it with fresh eyes by putting yourself in their shoes and trying to understand their histories, their motivations—in other words, by challenging your perspective. Can you give this other person the benefit of the doubt, as we never truly know what someone may be going through?

And remember, you have a choice here. Not every situation we confront needs to be a battle deserving of our limited energy. We need to learn to be choosy as we create a meaningful life.

Part C. The Power of Our Words

The words you speak become the house you live in.

~ Hafiz

Consider your words. Can the words you use shape your perception of reality? Can you reframe what is in front of you? Can the words you use help you see things more clearly?

Here are a couple of examples to consider:

- Cultivating a growth mindset (yes, Carol Dweck!) with the power of "yet."

  Instead of telling yourself you can't do it, tell yourself that you cannot do it … yet.

- Instead of saying "I have to," say "I get to."

  This is a suggestion that was shared with me by my positive psychology teacher, Emiliya Zhivotovskaya, and also cited in James Clear's book *Atomic Habits* (2018). Instead of seeing a task in front of us, such as folding clothes or washing dishes, as a chore, can we see the task as a privilege? Reflect on the power of this reframe. I am grateful to be living in a place I call home, that I own clothes that need to be washed and dishes that need to be cleaned. Instead of focusing on a list of nuisances/annoyances/troubles, can we focus on gratitude and acknowledge the many blessings and privileges in our lives? The next time you are late to class or a meeting, tell yourself that you *get* to join this class or meeting, and acknowledge the opportunity in front of you. Maybe you are a student or worker, and you have the opportunity to pursue an education or passion. Be curious about how you can tweak the words you use (i.e., adding "yet," and "I get to!") and potentially create tiny, cumulative shifts that will result in a more grateful and meaningful life.[19]

THE WHY

Is there evidence that challenging our perspective and our mind chatter can lead to benefits in our well-being? As discussed in the *Mind-Body Connection* section, psychotherapies such as Cognitive Behavioural Therapy (CBT), developed by Aaron Beck, have this aim. There is ample evidence to show that challenging our thinking in this way can have dramatic effects on how we act and feel. Of course, the relationship between these constructs is not

---

[19] I want to acknowledge the privilege in this suggestion. If you are currently in a situation in which you are struggling (financially, emotionally, physically, spiritually), can you acknowledge this struggle and reach out for support (possibly from family or friends, or resources in the community)? I recognize the struggles that many individuals within our communities experience, including poverty, prejudice and discrimination, inadequate community resources, or lack of access to resources. Even given these unique struggles, is there an opportunity for a potential reframe when it comes to even one or some of these challenges? Maybe, or maybe not; it is for you to decide.

unidirectional. Changing how we act and feel alters how we think as well. Each component affects *and* is affected by the other components. Beck used a triangle to represent this idea, as illustrated in Figure 12.

FIGURE 12: THE COGNITIVE TRIANGLE

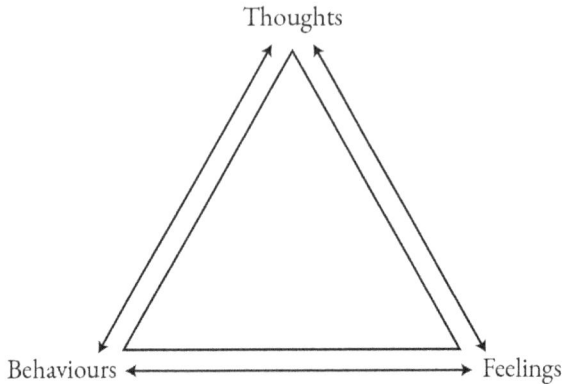

Thoughts

Behaviours ← → Feelings

CBT has been shown to be effective for a broad range of mental health issues, including anxiety and related disorders, and mood disorders (Hofmann et al., 2012).

THE HOW

And now is your opportunity to apply this new learning as you challenge your perspective and talk back to your mind chatter!

Exercise 1: Talking Back to Your Mind Chatter

Return to the thoughts/beliefs that you highlighted on page 72 and write each one down in the left column. In the right column, talk back to this thought/belief. For each one:

- Ask yourself, what evidence do I have that disproves this belief? Why is this thought/belief *not* true?

- Reflect on the three Ps (personal, pervasive, and permanent; refer to pages 75–76) as it relates to your thought/belief. Is it really all about you (personal), or are there other person(s) or situational factors that share some responsibility? Does nothing ever go right for you (pervasive), or are you selectively focusing on your perceived "misses" or "failures"? And will this never change (permanent), or can you envision the possibility that things can get better in the future?

ORIGINAL THOUGHT/BELIEF (MIND CHATTER)	TALKING BACK TO YOUR MIND CHATTER!

Exercise 2: Reframing a Difficult Situation/Event

Think about a situation or event that brings up a strong emotion for you. Be careful not to begin with a situation that is traumatizing.

Now ask yourself these questions (the ones that are applicable):

- Is there another way to see this situation? The first step is to acknowledge that this is only *one* perspective; most of the time, there are many ways of interpreting situations. If you cannot acknowledge this reality, I encourage you to engage in further reflection before moving on.

- Is this an obstacle/failure *or* a potential growth opportunity (growth mindset)?

- Is this a threat *or* challenge? Recall Kelly McGonigal's TED Talk *How to Make Stress Your Friend* (2013).

- What can I control or influence in this situation? We cannot control what other people say or do, but we do have control over our attitudes, how we think, and our behaviours, including effort and practice. If something is within your control or influence, what can you do now? Where do you want to direct your energy? Can you attempt to make amends with a friend, family member, or co-worker?

- Is there an opportunity to create much-needed space in my life and let something go or let it be? Recall the "Two Monks and a Woman Parable" on page 69.

Reflect on how these different lenses feel in your body. Do you soften when you consider the potential opportunity to learn, to grow, and to improve in the future? When faced with a challenging situation, this experience can highlight our core values, what is important to us, and help crystallize our priorities. In comparison, do you feel your body constrict and tighten when you view your situation with a lens of obstacle/barrier/failure/threat/blame/shame?

We can all benefit from self-compassion and forgiveness, either by directing that forgiveness toward yourself as you honour your humanness and the reality that we are all imperfect and make mistakes, or perhaps to another person who has harmed you in some way. Forgiving someone else has everything to do with *you*, and not them. As Jonathan Lockwood Huie reminds us, "Forgive others, not because they deserve forgiveness but because you deserve peace." This sentiment is echoed by the Buddhaghosa when he says, "Holding on to anger is like grasping a hot coal with the intent of throwing it at someone else; you are the one who gets burned." You do not need to express your forgiveness to this other person, but quietly doing so for yourself can help unburden you.

FOCUS BOX: "SALT IN A CUP VERSUS LAKE" PARABLE

(as cited in Shetty, 2020)

"What brings you to me?" asked an old, wise woman of the young man who stood before her. "I see joy and beauty around me, but from a distance," the young man said. "My own life is full of pain." The wise woman was silent. She slowly poured a cup of water for the sad young man and handed it to him. Then she held out a bowl of salt.

"Put some in the water," she said. The young man hesitated, then took a small pinch of salt. "More. A handful," the old woman said. Looking skeptical, the young man put a scoop of salt in his cup. The old woman gestured with her head, instructing the young man to drink. He took a sip of water, made a face, and spat it onto the dirt floor. "How was it?" the old woman asked. "Thanks, but no thanks," said the young man rather glumly.

The old woman smiled knowingly, then handed the young man the bowl of salt and led him to a nearby lake. The water was clear and cold. "Now put a handful of salt in the lake," she said. The young man did as he was instructed, and the salt dissolved into the water. "Have a drink," the old woman said. The young man knelt at the water's edge and slurped from his hands. When he looked up, the old woman again asked, "How was it?" "Refreshing," said the young man. "Could you taste the salt?" asked the wise woman. The young man smiled sheepishly. "Not at all," he said.

The old woman knelt next to the man, helped herself to some water, and said, "The salt is the pain of life. It is constant, but if you put it in a small glass, it tastes bitter. If you put it in a lake, you can't taste it. Expand your senses, expand your world, and the pain will diminish. Don't be the glass. Become the lake."

In this story, we are reminded of the power of perspective. Do we place our pain in a small container and suffocate as we become overwhelmed by our experience? Or do we step back and make much-needed space as we acknowledge other important aspects of our lives? The pain we experience, in whatever form, is a universal human experience; *we all will suffer*. Can we approach these difficult situations and emotions with compassion, holding space as we move through pain? And can our broader perspective ("the lake") help us realize that amid pain and suffering there are many things, experiences, and people in our lives to whom we are grateful? We will further explore these topics of gratitude and self-compassion in upcoming WOW tips (8 and 9 respectively). *Become the lake.*

WOW TIP 7:
MAKE MEANING AS YOU
CREATE EMPOWERING STORIES

*In some ways suffering ceases to be suffering at the moment
it finds a meaning, such as the meaning of a sacrifice.*

~ Viktor Frankl

THE WHAT & WHY

We have the power to create meaning. Our lives are not simply an accumulation of events. Finding meaning in the events we experience can empower us. Think about the perspective that we bring to a situation in which we may have been harmed, perhaps repeatedly. Do we tell our stories from the perspective of a victim or survivor? Think about these two words, and what each one feels like in your body. The events could be the same, but the stories we tell ourselves can change the way we feel about ourselves (our self-concept), what has happened, and our possibilities for the future. How do we string together these details? We have the power to shine a light (literally visualize a spotlight here) on the more empowering, calming, and uplifting experiences in our lives, and to minimize, omit, and reframe some of the more challenging situations.

A researcher that has done a lot of work in the field of "meaning making" is psychologist Michael Steger. Meaning is the "web of connections, understandings, and interpretations that help us *comprehend* our experience and *formulate plans* directing our energies to the achievement of our desired future" (Steger, 2012). In this definition, Steger highlights two aspects of meaning. The first is *coherence*, or the comprehension/understanding component; the part that illuminates the fact that our lives matter and make sense. The second component is *purpose*, the motivational element. It is the dynamic part of meaning, as we work toward goals that matter to us, he says (see *WOW Tip 13: Discover and Live Your Purpose* for further details). In a later publication, Martela and Steger (2016) add a third component to meaning: *significance*. It is the belief that one's life matters, or *existential mattering*. And to add to the complexity of this construct of meaning, more recently Hicks and Martela (2022) offer a fourth element: *experiential appreciation*, which "reflects the feeling of a deep connection to events as they transpire and the ability to extract value from that link. It represents the detection and admiration for life's inherent beauty."

One way of measuring "meaning" in our lives is by completing the Meaning of Life Questionnaire, created by Steger and his colleagues.

QUESTIONNAIRE 1: MEANING OF LIFE QUESTIONNAIRE

Abso-lutely Untrue	Mostly Untrue	Some-what Untrue	Can't Say True or False	Some-what True	Mostly True	Abso-lutely True
1	2	3	4	5	6	7
1. I understand my life's meaning.						
1	2	3	4	5	6	7
2. I am looking for something that makes my life more meaningful.						
1	2	3	4	5	6	7
3. I am always looking to find my life's purpose.						
1	2	3	4	5	6	7
4. My life has a clear sense of purpose.						
1	2	3	4	5	6	7
5. I have a good sense of what makes my life meaningful.						
1	2	3	4	5	6	7
6. I have discovered a satisfying life purpose.						
1	2	3	4	5	6	7
7. I am always searching for something that makes my life feel significant.						
1	2	3	4	5	6	7
8. I am seeking a purpose or mission for my life.						
1	2	3	4	5	6	7
9. My life has no clear purpose.						
1	2	3	4	5	6	7
10. I am searching for meaning in my life.						
1	2	3	4	5	6	7

Source: Adapted from Steger (2010); for more information and instructions for scoring, see this resource listed under References

Benefits of Finding Meaning

Making sense of our lives is related to an improved sense of well-being. For example, rewriting one's story after a stressful or traumatic event can be therapeutic. According to Steger (2012), "People's lives encompass more than what is happening now and trace an arc of experience that links one's past and present circumstances to one's future prospects and pursuits. People's ability to make sense of their lives should facilitate this sort of transcendence, enabling them to find a meaningful place for the things that happen to them, and in the world around them." Having a sense of meaning is linked to positive affect and emotions, global happiness, life satisfaction, positive self-empowering traits such as ego-resiliency and an internal locus of control, more desirable perspectives, and a better ability to manage challenges.

Making sense of our lives is also related to less psychological distress and psychopathology. According to Tedeschi and his colleagues (1998, as cited in Steger, 2012), enhanced meaning is often the result of enduring difficulties in life. Experiencing a challenging situation forces us to engage in this reflective exercise. Steger (2012) found that a higher sense of meaning is inversely related to negative affect and emotions, neuroticism, PTSD severity, depression, hostility, antisociality, aggression, hopelessness, and substance use.

James Pennebaker, a pioneer of expressive writing, has shown that doing expressive writing exercises for as little as 15 minutes a day for three days produces a host of benefits. According to Pennebaker and his colleagues (Pennebaker, 1997; Pennebaker & Chung, 2012), most participants find the exercise to be beneficial and meaningful, irrespective of age (children to elderly), sex (men and women), and topic (medical diagnosis, college entry, and traumas). Other benefits have been documented including physical (e.g., better immune and cardiovascular functioning) and behavioural (e.g., higher GPA, job re-employment, and reduced job absenteeism) benefits. Disclosing one's stories and associated emotions is liberating. In contrast, inhibition or keeping a problem or trauma a secret is stressful, as it increases cognitive load and is physically taxing. An alternative explanation is that the emergence of a coherent narrative over the course of writing sessions is the healing element. Making sense of our lives is what is driving these benefits.

Post-Traumatic Growth

*Adversity shakes the foundation of our character to see if
what we believe and value is really worth standing for.*

~ Rae Smith

No mud, no lotus.

~ Thích Nhất Hạnh

Post-traumatic stress disorder is a DSM-5 diagnosis that is precipitated by one's exposure to a traumatic event. Most of us are unaware of the possibility of post-traumatic growth (PTG), even though this reality is more common compared to PTSD following trauma.[20] For most survivors of trauma and other challenging events including bereavement, distress, if experienced, is transient. Resiliency is the most common outcome following a tragedy (Bonanno, 2004, 2021).

PTG, a concept coined by psychologists Richard Tedeschi and Lawrence Calhoun in 1995, is defined as "the experience of positive change that occurs as a result of the struggle with highly challenging life crises" (Tedeschi & Calhoun, 2004). It often coexists with psychological distress. In fact, according to these authors, "Growth, however, does not occur as a direct result of trauma. It is the individual's struggle with the new reality in the aftermath of trauma that is crucial in determining the extent to which post-traumatic growth occurs." It may also involve redefining themselves, in ways that include their identities and their goals. For example, if following a car accident a person experiences paraplegia, they will need to redefine their identity. How will this injury impact their work, their leisure, and their relationships?

According to Tedeschi and Calhoun (2004), there are five aspects of PTG:

1. *Increased appreciation for life:* Many survivors will often say that they see life as a "gift," and they appreciate the simple things in life, like hugging their child, a sunset, or a good meal.

2. *Changed priorities:* Many survivors claim that they have a new sense of priorities; for example, that work is not everything and family comes first.

---

[20] Important caveat: Please note that we all respond to trauma in unique ways. The research shows that various factors, including prior trauma, low social support, and hyperarousal, can increase one's likelihood of developing PTSD following trauma, and in no way should it be interpreted that individuals who develop PTSD are weak or flawed in any way.

3. *More meaningful interpersonal relationships:* Many survivors report that they now know the meaning of family and friendship; that it took a tragedy to realize the meaning of true friendship.

4. *Increased sense of personal strength:* Many survivors recognize their strength; they realize that they can deal with life's challenges. They gain perspective.

5. *Richer existential and spiritual life:* This enhanced sense of spirituality may or may not be religious in nature; religiosity and spirituality are related yet separate dimensions.

Job Crafting

An important aspect of our lives is our work, whether paid or unpaid. Engaging in meaningful work is associated with benefits for the individual, their team, and their organization. Think about the work you do, whether it is paid employment, a volunteer opportunity, or a caregiving role, and consider whether you envision this work as a job, a career, or a calling. Do you show up to work to receive a paycheque or some other external incentive (a job)? Or is your motivation more intrinsically motivated, as you are searching for opportunities to advance and learn (a career)? Or do you feel called to your work, as it serves a greater purpose and aligns with your values (a calling)? One of the misconceptions is that some jobs are more meaningful and purposeful than others. For example, we may believe that doctors saving lives may derive more meaning and purpose from their work than the custodians who are cleaning the hospital rooms. But in their research, Wrzesniewski and Dutton (2001) found that many individuals employed in positions that others might consider to be menial work had a high sense of purpose in their work. Some hospital custodians would cognitively craft and reframe their work as "healers," as they took care cleaning the rooms so that patients could recover. In contrast, the individuals directly involved in saving lives, the doctors performing the surgeries, may be driven to this work for ego or prestige, not purpose. The opportunity to create meaning in our lives is possible, regardless of the work we do.

A good example of this point is Candice Billups, a hospital custodian, who sees her work as a calling. She describes her work in the following way:

> I love patients, I love sick people. I have so much to offer sick people. Because when I don't feel good or when I have had to have had surgeries, the one thing that has gotten me through has been ... jokes,

just being pleasant, being upbeat and having a great attitude. And that's what I enjoy most about being here. It's so upbeat here … I consider it the "house of hope." And that's what I tell the patients and all the visitors. It's a house of hope (as cited in Amortegui, 2015).

Envisioning your work as a calling and aligned to your purpose (your *why*) is associated with the most benefits. By definition, *job crafting* refers to the "active changes employees make to their own job designs in ways that can bring about numerous positive outcomes, including engagement, job satisfaction, resilience and thriving" (Berg et al., 2008). According to Wrzesniewski, Dutton, and their colleagues (Berg et al., 2008; Wrzesniewski & Dutton, 2001), job crafting involves changing one or more of the following elements:

1. *Task Crafting:* Changing what or how you do your job. For example, individuals can choose to do more or less of the tasks assigned to them, broaden or diminish the scope of the tasks, or actually change how the tasks are performed.

2. *Relational Crafting:* Changing the relationships one engages in at work. For example, this may involve changing the quality and/or amount of interaction one has with their colleagues. Remember, emotions are contagious. Working with toxic colleagues can be detrimental to your well-being; in contrast, working with engaged colleagues can be invigorating and productive.

3. *Cognitive Crafting:* Changing how one perceives their work. In other words, individuals are not necessarily changing what they do or their relationships; instead, they are changing how they perceive these aspects. They may reframe their jobs in some way (e.g., "healers" versus "cleaners"). In another example, legal aid lawyers reframed their jobs as work that "protects the right of all citizens to a fair trial" rather than "helping the criminals avoid condemnation." It's the same work, but the meaning that is assigned to their work differs.

Benefits of Job Crafting

Job crafting increases the meaning individuals find in their work and positively impacts their work identity (Wrzesniewski & Dutton, 2001). Meaningful work is also linked with increased job and life satisfaction and even less depression (Steger et al., 2013, as cited in Weir, 2013). A more engaged workforce will benefit the organization, from increased productivity and innovation to a more positive work culture as well. One caveat is that individuals will benefit from some degree of job crafting, but it may not be applicable or recommended for everyone. If you find yourself in a work situation that is not a good fit, such as when your work does not draw upon your strengths, or you are part of a toxic work environment, the best choice for you may be to move on. If you choose to stay, set clear boundaries so that you do not become overwhelmed. Be your own advocate!

THE HOW

Expressive Writing

Here are the general instructions for expressive writing. Choose a topic, ranging from a stressful event (e.g., starting college) to a trauma (e.g., near-death experience). Start with a less-stressful event and work your way up to writing about more difficult experiences. Write for as little as 15 minutes per day, for three to four days.

EXPRESSIVE WRITING EXERCISE

Instructions from Pennebaker (1997) and Pennebaker and Chung (2012):

"Write about your very deepest thoughts and feelings about the most traumatic experience of your entire life. In your writing, I'd like you to really let go and explore your very deepest emotions and thoughts. You might tie your topic to your relationships with others, including parents, lovers, friends, or relatives, to your past, your present, or your future, or to who you have been, who you would like to be, or who you are now. You may write about the same general issues or experiences on all days of writing or on different traumas each day."

Job Crafting

Reflect on the three aspects of job crafting—task crafting, relational crafting, and cognitive crafting—as they relate to your work (paid or unpaid). Are there any tweaks that can be made?

Task Crafting: Changing what or how you do your job. E.g., individuals can choose to do more or less of the tasks assigned to them, broaden or diminish the scope of the tasks, or change how the tasks are performed.	
Relational Crafting: Changing the relationships one engages in at work. E.g., this may involve changing the quality and/or amount of interaction one has with their colleagues.	
Cognitive Crafting: Changing how one perceives their work. In other words, individuals are not necessarily changing what they do or their relationships; instead, they are changing how they perceive these aspects. They may reframe their jobs in some way (e.g., I am a "healer," not a "cleaner").	

WOW TIP 8: CULTIVATE GRATITUDE

THE WHAT

According to gratitude researchers Emmons and Shelton (2002), gratitude is a "felt sense of wonder, thankfulness and appreciation for life." Emmons (2010) says it consists of two components:

1. An affirmation of goodness; the acknowledgement that there is good in our lives.

2. An inference that someone in our lives or a spiritual being is responsible for this goodness or "gift." Thus, there is an "other focus" to gratitude.

Can you find gratitude in your day, perhaps for good health, mobility, educational opportunities, a secure home, family, and/or friends? Or maybe smaller things—a warm cup of coffee, someone holding the door, or a friendly smile? We can also be grateful that something negative has *not* happened to us.

THE WHY

According to Emmons (2010), there are many benefits of being grateful, including:

- *Physical Benefits:* stronger immune systems, being less bothered by aches and pains, lower blood pressure, exercising more and taking better care of our health, sleeping longer, and feeling more refreshed upon awakening

- *Psychological Benefits:* higher levels of positive emotions, feeling more alert, alive, and awake, experiencing more joy and pleasure, and experiencing more optimism and happiness

- *Social Benefits:* being more helpful, generous, and compassionate, being more forgiving, more outgoing, and less lonely and isolated

THE HOW

In the space below, write down 10 things that you are grateful for, big or small, and why you are grateful for each item.

1. I am grateful for _____
    because _____

2. I am grateful for _____
    because _____

3. I am grateful for _____
    because _____

4. I am grateful for _____
    because _____

5. I am grateful for _____
    because _____

6. I am grateful for _____
    because _____

7. I am grateful for _____
    because _____

8. I am grateful for _____
    because _____

9. I am grateful for _____
    because _____

10. I am grateful for _____
    because _____

Some other gratitude exercises to consider:

- *Keep a gratitude journal* and write down three things that you are grateful for each day. To lend support to this intervention, Seligman and his colleagues (2005) asked participants to write down three things that went well each day and their causes every night for one week. They then measured their happiness and depression levels immediately following the intervention, and then again at one-week and one-, three-, and six-month intervals. In general, participants showed higher happiness levels and decreased depressive symptoms at each of these points, compared to the control group. Further, in a series of experiments, Emmons and McCullough (2003) found that there were personal and/or relational benefits for counting one's blessings versus hassles, neutral life events, or social comparisons. The impact on one's positive affect was one of the most pronounced impacts revealed in this study.

- *Keep a gratitude jar or board* in a communal space in your home or at the lunch table at work. Encourage others to write gratitude lists in the jar and watch them grow, or write gratitude messages on the board, perhaps even thanking someone in your shared space.

- *Write a gratitude letter.* If the person is still living, consider reading it to them and leaving a copy—a boost of happiness for both the sender and receiver! Seligman and his colleagues (2005) tested this exercise, the Gratitude Visit, against four other happiness interventions—Three Good Things in Life, You at Your Best, Using Signature Strengths in a New Way, and Identifying Signature Strengths—and one control exercise. They found that the Gratitude Visit provided the largest boost in happiness up to a one-month follow-up visit. For further instructions on this exercise, go to the Greater Good in Action website: https://ggia.berkeley.edu/practice/gratitude_letter.

- *Use primers.* In our home, we have a gratitude rock, a smooth rock with the word *gratitude* etched in it, sitting on our sink in our main washroom. Every time I wash my hands, I think about one thing that I am grateful for.

- *Do a gratitude meditation.* You might try Sam Harris's three-minute meditation on YouTube or the one offered on the Greater Good in Action (GGIA) website.

WOW TIP 9:
PRACTICE SELF-COMPASSION

Talk to yourself like you would to someone you love.

~ Brené Brown

A moment of self-compassion can change your entire day.
A string of such moments can change the course of your life.

~ Christopher Germer

THE WHAT

In the words of Kristen Neff (n.d.-a), a self-compassion expert, author of *Self-Compassion* and *Fierce Self-Compassion*, and creator of the website selfcompassion.org:

> Having compassion for yourself means that you honor and accept your humanness. Things will not always go the way you want them to. You will encounter frustrations, losses will occur, you will make mistakes, bump up against your limitations, fall short of your ideals. This is the human condition, a reality shared by all of us. The more you open your heart to this reality instead of constantly fighting against it, the more you will be able to feel compassion for yourself and all your fellow humans in the experience of life.

According to Neff (n.d.-a), there are three components to self-compassion:

- *Self-kindness:* When we accept the fact that life includes failure, disappointment, and imperfection, we can have a softer response to these experiences.

- *Common humanity:* There is comfort in knowing that we *all* suffer—vulnerability, failure, and imperfection are part of the human experience. This realization diminishes the isolation we may feel if we believe that we alone have these experiences.

- *Mindfulness:* Mindfulness means being open and nonjudgmental to our experience, observing our thoughts and feelings as they occur and not over-identifying with them.

At the core of self-compassion is acceptance. We have evolved to resist or avoid physical discomfort. Remember that our limbic system, the emotional part of our brain, aims to keep us safe. Unfortunately, this inclination, while making us more comfortable, is counterproductive. As suggested in Carl Jung's "What you resist, persists," resisting emotional suffering feeds a challenging emotion. Likewise, expressing emotion by yelling or hitting a punching bag feeds the emotion; the scientific literature shows little support for catharsis theory, as expressing anger *increases* one's anger! So, if we shouldn't resist this emotion or express it, what should we do? The research shows that we should lean into the emotion and move through it with self-compassion. Although there are many methods for working with tough emotions, psychologist and meditation teacher Tara Brach's RAIN method, featured in her book *Radical Compassion*, offers one tool for bringing mindfulness and self-compassion into our conscious experience (Brach, 2020b):

R: Recognize What's Going On

A: Allow the Experience to be There, Just as It Is

I: Investigate with Interest and Care

N: Nurture with Self-Compassion

Note: At the end of this chapter, I will share my own "eclectic" method of working with challenging emotions, borrowing ideas from mindfulness, self-compassion, and CBT.

THE WHY

There are many benefits for cultivating self-compassion. Self-compassion is linked to lower cortisol levels and higher heart rate variability (Neff, n.d.-e). These biochemical changes are associated with less stress and better cardiovascular functioning. In an interview (Marsh, 2012), Neff discussed her findings that self-compassionate individuals report less depression and greater optimism, happiness, and life satisfaction. Further, they demonstrate better self-care: they are more likely to exercise, eat a healthier diet, engage in more frequent doctor visits, and engage in safer sex! Additionally, there is a motivational benefit to being self-compassionate, as it is related to being more likely to pursue positive change (Breines & Chen, 2012, as cited in McGonigal, 2012). Many of us have the belief that we need to be tough on ourselves to make strides in life. But beating yourself up after a perceived failure makes it *less* likely that you will work toward your goals! Instead, be kind to yourself, see this setback as a learning opportunity, and move on. Reflect on what happened and consider what you can do differently in the future.

Beyond the individual-level benefits, self-compassion improves social relationships, as self-compassionate individuals are kinder and more generous with their partners (Marsh, 2012). This relational benefit is likely bidirectional in nature. When we are kinder to ourselves when faced with difficult situations and emotions, the kinder we are to others. In turn, being more compassionate with others and giving them the benefit of the doubt leads us to be gentler with ourselves. Showing up this way in our relationships with others also makes it more likely that our kindness will be reciprocated.

THE HOW

There are multiple ways that we can cultivate self-compassion. Christopher Germer, in his book *The Mindful Path to Self-Compassion* (2009), highlights five pathways: physical, mental, emotional, relational, and spiritual. Here are a few strategies that focus on the body, affect (emotion), and mind … BAM! As an alternative, explore Tara Brach's RAIN method, as previously suggested.

Body

When dealing with a challenging situation or distressing emotion, start with grounding the body. Notice what is happening in your body and breathe, taking slow, relaxed breaths, ideally with exhales longer than the inhales. If you feel comfortable, put one hand on your heart and the other on your belly, and feel your chest and belly expand on your inhale and contract on your exhale. If you do not find the breath to be calming, listen to your body and find something that is grounding for you, such as repeating a kind word or phrase, or visualizing a loved one or special place. Especially if you are in an agitated state, find an object of focus that can ground you into the present moment.

In addition, you may choose to warm your body. Recall the studies reported in the *Mind-Body Connection* section (refer to page 28) that suggest that there is a link between physical warmth and psychological warmth (for a summary, see Bargh & Melnikoff, 2019). These studies suggest that physical warmth, elicited by holding something warm versus cold, promotes kindness, an aspect of psychological warmth. The next time you are feeling distressed, offer yourself the same kindness you would offer to your family or friends when they are struggling, and consider starting with a little warmth, like a warm cup of tea or a cozy blanket.

Affect (Emotion)

Befriend your emotions. Lean in and label your emotion by saying, "This is anxiety," or "This is anger." There is research that shows that labelling our emotions, whether it be fear, anger, or disgust, actually calms the brain (Lieberman et al., 2007). This finding offers an additional reason why expressive writing exercises can be so powerful. In fact, labelling emotions increases activity in a part of the prefrontal cortex, the evolutionarily newer and "rational/logical/thinking" part of the brain, and decreases activity in the amygdala, part of the limbic system and the evolutionarily older and "emotional" part of the brain. This cascade of neural changes leads to a decrease in distress and overwhelm, as one is less likely to be hijacked by these emotions. Try to remain curious as you engage in this task. There is research to show that different emotions are indistinguishable at a physiological level. For example, both anxiety and excitement show up in similar ways—autonomic nervous system arousal. Is it possible that what you instinctively label as anxiety may be something else? Can a simple reframe change how you feel about your body revving up before delivering a presentation? For example, "This is not a threat but a challenge," or "It is not something *I have to* do, but something *I get to* do." Kelly McGonigal's (2013) TED Talk, *How to Make Stress Your Friend* (I alluded to this talk earlier on page 29), and *WOW Tip 6: Challenge Your Perspective and Mind Chatter* may provide some additional reframes.

Mind

And finally, consider repeating some mindful phrases or mantras to yourself. Here are some mantras for your consideration:

- This too shall pass.
- Breathe in, breathe out, move on.
- Just keep swimming.
- All is well.

Before I leave this topic, here are some other self-compassion exercises to consider:

Exercise 1: Self-Compassion Journal (Neff, n.d.-d)

Kristen Neff recommends keeping a self-compassion journal as a means of experiencing both physical and psychological benefits. At the end of your day, reflect on the events experienced and then focus on ones that may have caused you discomfort or pain. For each event, reflect on the three components of self-compassion—self-kindness, common humanity, and mindfulness—as you try to process this event in a self-compassionate way. Remind yourself that you are human, and that we all make mistakes. Instead of beating yourself up about what has happened, is there an opportunity to lean in with self-compassion? Can you adopt a growth mindset and see a learning opportunity and/or offer an apology for any wrongdoing? When we approach these situations with kindness, we are more willing to grow from our experiences, rather than being defensive and steeping in challenging emotions.

Exercise 2: How Would You Treat a Friend? (Neff, n.d.-b)

We often respond to our friends' suffering with more compassion than we do for ourselves. Think about a difficult situation that you may be experiencing. Now imagine that it is your friend that is telling you about this same difficulty in their life. What would you say to them? Now say it to yourself!

A variant of this exercise is the Self-Compassionate Letter (Greater Good in Action, n.d.). Once you have identified something that makes you feel inadequate or "less than," identify the emotions that come up just as they are. Then write a self-compassionate letter to yourself. For further information about this exercise, visit the GGIA website.

MY SELF-COMPASSIONATE LETTER

Dear _____ (your name here),

Exercise 3: Loving-Kindness Meditation

When exploring *WOW Tip 5: Cultivate Mindfulness*, we highlighted the benefits of engaging in mindful meditation. An increasing body of research shows similar advantages for practicing a loving-kindness meditation (LKM or *metta*), which aims to enhance kindness toward oneself and others. Some of the benefits of a LKM include increased positive emotions and decreased challenging ones, enhanced feelings of social connection, and decreased chronic pain (Seppälä, 2014). Fredrickson and her colleagues (2008) conducted a study in which participants kept a daily LKM practice for nine weeks. At the end of this intervention, they experienced benefits that included building of their cognitive, emotional, and physical resources. According to these authors:

> The practice of LKM led to shifts in people's daily experiences of a wide range of positive emotions, including love, joy, gratitude, contentment, hope, pride, interest, amusement, and awe. These increases in positive emotions were evident both within the trajectories of change in daily emotions over the span of 9 weeks and within a detailed analysis of a given morning 2 weeks after formal training ended. These shifts in positive emotions took time to appear and were not large in magnitude, but over the course of 9 weeks, they were linked to increases in a variety of personal resources, including mindful attention, self-acceptance, positive relations with others, and good physical health. Moreover, these gains in personal resources were consequential: They enabled people to become more satisfied with their lives and to experience fewer symptoms of depression. Simply put, by elevating daily experiences of positive emotions, the practice of LKM led to long-term gains that made genuine differences in people's lives.

Here I will provide you with a few metta meditation options. I will use the words of Roshi Joan Halifax (2009) to frame this practice for us: *Strong back, soft front.* Let us reflect on what these words are conveying to us:

- *Strong back:* Can we be grounded in a strong foundation, greeting our challenging experiences with the grace of courage and bravery?

- *Soft front:* When confronted with discomfort, whether it be fear, anger, or frustration, can we soften around the hard edges of these emotions and embrace this experience of suffering?

By grounding ourselves in the present moment, can these emotions soften, the edges become a little less jagged, as we learn to ride its waves? Find a comfortable seated position and follow these instructions:

Step 1. Start by lengthening your spine and rolling your shoulders back as your shoulder blades gently move toward each other. By doing so, you can create an open heart. *Strong back, soft front.*

Step 2. Take a deep breath in … and an extended breath out. You may choose to put one hand on your chest and another on your belly as you take two or three more relaxing breaths. If breath is not a way for you to find some relaxation in your body, use an object of focus that works for you. It could be a kind word or phrase, such as "love," "gratitude," "all is well," or "I am enough," or it could be visualizing a loved one, a pet, or a special place. Listen to your body and find something that works for you.

Step 3. When you are ready, recite one of the following metta meditations:

Option 1 (Yang, 2021)

> *May I be loving, open, and aware in this moment;*
> *If I cannot be loving, open, and aware in this moment, may I be kind;*
> *If I cannot be kind, may I be nonjudgmental;*
> *If I cannot be nonjudgmental, may I not cause harm;*
> *If I cannot not cause harm, may I cause the least harm possible.*

Option 2: Self-compassionate break (Neff, n.d.-c)

> *May I give myself the compassion that I need.*
> *May I learn to accept myself as I am.*
> *May I forgive myself.*
> *May I be strong.*
> *May I be patient.*

Option 3: For "caretakers," those who serve others as parents, children of aging parents, teachers, or support workers (Halifax, 2018)

> *May I offer my care and presence unconditionally, knowing it may be met by gratitude, indifference, anger or anguish.*
> *May I offer love, knowing that I cannot control the course of life, suffering, or death.*
> *May I find the inner resources to truly be able to give.*
> *May I be peaceful and let go of expectations.*
> *May I accept things as they are.*
> *May I see my limits compassionately, just as I view the suffering of others.*

For other loving-kindness meditation (LKM) options, go to Kristen Neff's website (https://www.selfcompassion.org) and click on the Practices tab, and choose Guided Meditations. Alternatively, visit Barbara Fredrickson's website for her book *Love 2.0*, https://www.positivityresonance.com, and click on the Meditations tab. The first meditation listed is the one for loving-kindness. Sharon Salzberg, world-renowned meditation teacher and author of *Lovingkindness*, has written extensively on this topic and has many guided LKM meditations online.

FOCUS BOX: WORKING WITH CHALLENGING EMOTIONS— AN INTEGRATION OF MINDFULNESS, COGNITIVE STRATEGIES, AND SELF-COMPASSION

My method of working with challenging emotions is eclectic; I combine elements from various methodologies, some that may appear to be contradictory on the surface. Here are my two simple steps that I cycle through repeatedly, as I return to step 1 throughout my practice:

Step 1. Ground yourself in the present moment.

For most of us, that means coming back to our breath—see *WOW Tip 1: Breathe*, or another Focus Out strategy—noting what you can see, hear, feel, taste, or smell in your external environment. Once you feel settled, move to the next step.

Step 2. Feel the feeling (option to label the emotion as well).

This means leaning into an uncomfortable sensation(s), which is counter to our initial inclinations to resist pain or discomfort. As a suggestion, use UM's See-Hear-Feel mindfulness technique (refer to page 65) to disentangle your emotional experience: Where are you feeling this emotion most strongly in your body? What mental images or mental talk are arising in this moment? Can you bring an equanimous response to these arisings, in both your mind and body? Do your best to follow Pema Chödrön's advice: *Feel the feeling, drop the story.* Dropping the story or narrative can be a challenge, because we are so easily drawn into these storylines, including "I am not enough," "here we go again," "I am not worthy," and shame themes such as "it is *my* fault" or blame themes such as "it is *your* fault." These stories, which we so easily weave, often intensify our emotional experience. Can you recognize and acknowledge these threads, and then have equanimity with them as you drop the story? Can you acknowledge the chatter and not give it weight? In the words of Allan Lokos, "Don't believe everything that you think. Thoughts are just that—thoughts." The problem is not the emotion but your *struggle* with the emotion, your attempts at resistance—"the push"—and our attachments and grasping—"the pull." Equanimity, a core ingredient of mindfulness, does not involve this push/pull. As you begin to let go of one storyline, can you begin to weave another, one that is grounded in self-compassion? Can you start to change your narrative, and bring softness to this rewrite? Start with self-compassionate phrases, such as "I am enough," "I am worthy," and "I am a good person and sometimes I make mistakes." Observe how these statements resonate in your body and be curious as to where this story takes you.

I have experienced very intense emotions, primarily anxiety, for most of my life. And as I have deepened my mindfulness practice, I have brought a curious "beginner's mind" to each of these experiences, becoming an explorer, or detective of sorts. As I begin to explore any intense emotion, I first pause and breathe deeply as I aim to notice where I feel it most strongly. For me, I feel warmth and heaviness in my chest area. I try to ground myself in the present moment by putting my hand to my chest, the location where I feel the emotion most intensely, and bring my attention to my feet on the floor. In my mind, I may name the emotion "anxiety," either at this stage or at a later point in my internal exploration, and then I sit back and observe what is happening, moment to moment, until it fades, as it will! I track the change and movement in this *feel* space as I recognize the impermanence of the experience. *Nothing lasts forever. This too shall pass ... and IS passing.* If what I am feeling in my body becomes more intense, I anchor back to my breath, and bring attention to the grounding sensations in my body— my feet on the floor or my back against the chair. And when those thoughts pop up (as they will multiple times), I acknowledge them until they begin to fade. I sometimes envision these thoughts tied to passing clouds floating away. My only aim in the moment is to observe whatever it is that comes up in my mind and body. Without judgment. With expansive equanimity.

One final suggestion: When you are not feeling so emotionally charged, you can start to challenge your mind chatter and engage in some strategies that were provided in *WOW Tip 6: Challenge Your Perspective and Mind Chatter*. This strategy may appear to counter the aims of mindfulness. Mindfulness, including mindfulness-based approaches such as Acceptance and Commitment Therapy (ACT), involves having equanimity with our thoughts and not engaging in the push/pull. A cognitive strategy like talking back to your mind chatter, a key component of Cognitive Behavioural Therapy (CBT), involves this form of engagement. I have made gains with a CBT approach, as it has helped me gain perspective when working with challenging emotions. But there is sometimes "residue." No matter how much I engage in this process, and even if I have evidence for why this problematic thought is *not* true, I can still feel some intense emotions; there is a disconnect between my cognitions and the visceral reaction I feel in my body. To work with this experience, I have found that a more mindful approach that emphasizes equanimity has served me well. Please consider my suggestions throughout this book as offerings; remember, you have choices, and you will decide what you need to do in each moment. Instead of staying with an intense emotion, and possibly oscillating between turning toward or anchoring away from these reactions and judgments, you may need something different, like a brisk walk or run, or a comforting phone call with a friend. Acknowledge that you are building a toolbox for yourself, and choose the tools that are most appropriate for you as you customize your approach. Although I generally come back to this general sequence (as outlined above) when I work with challenging emotions, I know that I utilize different strategies from time to time. I hope you can learn to do the same for yourself.

WOW TIP 10:
BECOME MORE TIME AFFLUENT

THE WHAT

According to Ashley Whillans, author of *Time Smart* (2020), time affluence is "the state of having and using time meaningfully." We need to value and prioritize our time and energy over other things like money and possessions that we wrongfully assume are more strongly tied to our happiness and well-being. We need to start living our lives for today, and value the precious time we have. As Whillans explains, "Time poverty doesn't necessarily arise from a mismatch between the hours we have and the hours we need. It results from how we *think about* and *value* those hours. It's as much psychological as it is structural. We might not be working more hours, but we are making decisions to work at all hours. We are ceaselessly connected."

Research has shown that although there are many benefits to being more time centric, there are several barriers. Whillans identifies six time traps that can lead to time poverty.

1. *Technology:* The paradox is that technology saves us time, but it also takes it away and fragments the precious time we have into tiny bits we lose throughout the day, weeks, and years. Brigid Schulte, author of *Overwhelmed* (2015), refers to these tiny snippets as *time confetti—* the seconds it takes to check a text, an email, or a notification add up. This loss of focus has big costs, she explains, in terms of productivity and overall happiness. By taking attention away from the task with technology, we waste time by engaging in these "checking" activities and then re-engaging with our primary task.

2. *Money focus:* As a culture, we have been taught that money equals happiness. Although recent research shows that there is a relationship between money and happiness, prioritizing money over other contributors to our health and well-being does not serve us well. Chasing wealth is a trap.

3. *Undervalued time:* There are many examples of how we undervalue our time. Are you likely to drive a couple of additional kilometers to save a few cents per litre on gas? Are you likely to purchase a connecting flight and extend your travel time to save a few hundred dollars instead

of buying a direct flight for more money? Many of us unconsciously go for the lowest cost when doing so can increase our stress and fatigue. Think about this time-money trade-off when making future decisions. Is it worth saving a few extra dollars?

4. *Busyness as status:* Increasingly, many people prioritize their work over their family and friends to find purpose, and wear their "busyness" as a badge of honour. Until recently, I fell into this trap. I found I was always connected with my work, to the detriment of other things that matter to me. My relationships with those close to me are of utmost importance, but until recently I was tied to my computer and worked toward perfection in almost everything I did as it was never *good enough.* I acknowledge that much of my identity is tied to my role as a teacher, and I take great pride in teaching and fostering relationships with my students. But many times, I am left feeling that I am a bad parent, partner, or friend. Writing this book has given me an opportunity to shift my priorities, to work toward setting clearer boundaries for myself as I learn to accept "good enough." Instead of viewing my focus on time affluence as some sort of laziness, I need to reframe my focus on self and relationships as much-needed "energy management." Now that sounds better!

5. *Idleness aversion:* There is always something that can be cleaned, wiped, folded, typed, or organized! I get it—I have a hard time relaxing too. But I am learning to be more mindful and to make time to do nothing, a quest that I would not have been interested in undertaking prior to diving into the research on positive psychology, and more specifically the benefits of mindfulness. Give your mind a break—disconnect from technology and other activities that zap your energy. Again, it is not laziness. (Reframe, reframe, reframe!)

6. *Planning fallacy:* We tend to underestimate how much time any future task will take. We incorrectly assume that we will have more time tomorrow than we do today. Be selective when saying yes, and be sure to add much-needed free space in your calendar that can be incorporated between meetings and appointments, or simply at the start or end of each day. Don't be tempted to pack your calendar by scheduling back-to-back activities. Make time for—and savour—this downtime, ideally free from technology and other mind-consuming distractions.

So how many of these barriers apply to your situation? You will need to reflect on the ones that resonate with you if you are hoping to become more time affluent.

THE WHY

This advice to focus on time over money seems to be common sense, but perhaps a luxury available only to those who are privileged financially. But as Whillans highlights in *Time Smart* (2020), it is imperative that all of us, especially those who may be struggling financially, put a premium on our time and make decisions and trade-offs that reflect our focus on time over money. Benefits associated with time affluence are that it promotes:

- *Happiness:* Simply put, time-affluent people are happier!

- *Social connections:* Social connectedness is crucial for overall well-being. It is not only our relationships with our family, friends, and co-workers that matter, but also our brief interactions with strangers—in line at the grocery store, at the bus stop, or at the park. Don't underestimate these brief interactions; they can provide you with a boost to your happiness.

- *Relationship satisfaction:* Interestingly, time-focused individuals report higher relationship satisfaction with their spouses and better sex lives! In fact, Whillans's research showed that time-saving purchases, such as hiring a house cleaner can enhance your relationship satisfaction.

- *Job satisfaction:* It is not that individuals who are time centric work less than those who value money, as they tend to work the same number of hours. The difference is that the former group tends to pursue careers they love, leading to less stress and more productivity and creativity.

- *Prosocial behaviour:* Individuals who are time centric are more likely to serve others in various capacities, such as volunteering.

THE HOW

Whillans (2020) has organized the ways of becoming more time affluent into three strategies:

1. *Find time.* Spend more time on activities that bring you joy, and less time on activities that do not. When possible, schedule active leisure activities such as volunteering, socializing, and moving your body over passive leisure activities such as watching TV, scrolling through Instagram, and online shopping. Here are some suggestions:

- When waiting in line or commuting to work, make these activities more enjoyable by listening to music, an audiobook, or a podcast.

- Set boundaries on your use of technology (more about this topic in *WOW Tip 11: Create a New Relationship with Your Tech Devices*).

- Savour your meals. You can derive joy from cooking a great meal and then feasting on your creation. If you do not enjoy cooking, you may want to explore options with meal prep delivery kits, search online for an easy recipe, eat out, or order in. Either way, plan to enjoy your meals with your family or friends, when possible.

- Find time to experience *awe*. Can you be mindful in your experiences, engage your senses, and take in what is around you more fully? You can derive awe from various activities—hiking on a trail and taking in the incredible surroundings, immersing yourself in a concert, taking in great works of art at a museum, or watching children, animals, or both interacting with one another. To experience awe, simply slow down and pay attention to the vastness that surrounds us; acknowledge that we are part of something larger than us. For some, this experience of awe may be tied to transcendence and/or spirituality, whether there is a religious aspect to it or not.

2. *Fund time.* Outsource as much work as possible. Even if you are on a tight budget, are there ways that you can fund time? Be creative—perhaps some of your options may have no or little cost. Remember, you don't need to do everything! If you are a single parent, can you connect with other caregivers and create opportunities to help each other out? Perhaps each parent can rotate caregiving responsibilities, leaving a couple of afternoons per month that you are child-free so that you can schedule some much-needed self-care time. Consider getting together and socializing with these parents as you collectively share caregiving responsibilities at a local park.

3. *Reframe time.* Instead of approaching your upcoming weekend as simply "the weekend," reframe it as a "holiday." What other possibilities can you think of?

WOW TIP 11:
CREATE A NEW RELATIONSHIP
WITH YOUR TECH DEVICES

THE WHAT

The goal is to have a better relationship with our tech devices. Reflect on how reliant you are on your technology—all of it, not just your cell phone—and think about how your engagement with each of these devices makes you feel. Does it add to your well-being and happiness, or subtract from it? What are you accessing? How are you using social media, and for what purpose? Are you consuming feel-good stories and connecting with family and friends to share photos and stories, or are you engaging in more problematic behaviours on these social media platforms, such as perfecting your social image, chasing the "likes" and other affirmations, and taking part in or being the recipient of bullying behaviours? Also, consider how much you are using your technology. Most people underestimate how much time they spend on their cell phones and devices. Acknowledge that the more time we spend interacting with our phones and other devices, the less time we have to explore and engage in other wellness-enhancing activities such as exercising, meeting up with friends, and meditating. Engaging in these reflective exercises with respect to the quantity and quality of our tech interactions will allow you to set goals for yourself when it comes to your relationship with these devices. The goal is to create choice when it comes to technology, not to become a slave to it.

THE WHY

There is cumulating research to support the claim that excessive cell phone and other tech device usage has detrimental consequences on our well-being. An increasing number of individuals across the lifespan are reporting that they are consumed with their technology. For many of us, our cell phones are the first thing we look at in the morning and the last thing we look at in the evening. In a recent survey, one-third of Americans said that they would rather give up sex for a year than their phones! And as we have already highlighted, hearing the "pings" of our phones can stimulate the same brain areas—the dopaminergic reward pathways—that are activated when a person sees stimuli related to their drug addiction. It is not surprising that the experience of phantom phone vibrations, falsely perceiving that one's devices are vibrating when they are not, is becoming an increasingly more common phenomenon. In fact, a study by Drouin and her colleagues (2012) found that almost 90%

of their undergraduate sample of 290 students experienced these phantom vibrations, at a frequency of about once every two weeks on average.

In this section, we will explore the impacts of excessive tech usage.

Mental Health

Depression and suicide-related outcomes, including contemplation, attempts, and completed suicides: Jean Twenge, author of *iGen* and *Generation Me,* has been at the forefront of this research showing the relationship between screen time, particularly social media and smart phone usage, and a host of mental health-related symptoms including depression and suicide-related outcomes among today's youth. Critics have pointed out that some of the research is correlational, meaning that they look at relationships between variables. Correlation does *not* mean causation. When we see a relationship between two variables—as in this case, cell phone usage and mental health symptomatology, where increased usage (variable A) is associated with increased mental health symptoms (variable B)—we cannot conclude that A leads to B. It is possible that the relationship is in the other direction, and an increase in mental health symptoms leads to increased usage, or other variables may account for the observed relationship. This point is valid, as one cannot conclude causation from correlational data. But there are other details that collectively support the claim that the relationship is a causal one (not excluding the hypothesis that other factors of course play a role in the increase in mental health issues today, and the acknowledgement that the *type* of online engagement is an important variable for consideration). According to Twenge (2020):

- Various longitudinal studies published in top-tiered journals rule out the proposition that mental health issues lead to tech overuse. The available evidence supports the claim that excessive tech use *causes* mental health symptoms.

- Other variables, including anxiety about climate change, income inequality, and student debt, cannot account for the rising mental health issues among youth that began around 2012. For example, both income inequality and student loan debt remained fairly constant around this time period. What changed around 2012 is the popularity and usage frequency of smartphones and various social media platforms. Interestingly, the link between digital usage and well-being is stronger among girls (compared to boys), as online activity appears to vary by gender; girls are more likely to spend time on smartphones and social media whereas boys are more likely to engage in gaming, a relatively less problematic online activity (Twenge & Martin, 2020).

Possible psychological impacts from online engagement, especially with social media, show that certain types of activities are more harmful than others, including editing and perfecting photographs and profiles, scrolling through posts with an emphasis on idealized lives and bodies ("upward" comparisons), chasing the "likes" on posts, and doomscrolling (consuming negative news stories online). Engaging in other social activities online may in fact contribute to better mental health outcomes if these activities help build community and strengthen one's sense of belonging. Thus, I would caution that any claims that simplify the relationship between these factors should be subject to scrutiny.

Loneliness: Is this online activity, especially interactions on social media platforms, linked to loneliness? A recent study by Melissa Hunt and her colleagues (2018) suggests that there is a causal link between these factors, whereby limiting one's time spent on social media, including Facebook, Snapchat, and Instagram, to no more than 10 minutes per day, per platform, decreased one's scores in loneliness and depression. Interestingly, these effects were especially significant for those who scored higher in depression at the onset of the study. The design of the study had advantages compared to past studies on the topic (i.e., experimental design versus survey, and an objective measure of social media usage obtained from usage data versus retrospective self-report).

Body image: There is growing concern about the relationship between social media, body dissatisfaction, and disordered eating. Although we are in an early stage of this research, and many of the studies conducted thus far are correlational in nature, there is evidence to suggest that posting and editing photos and profiles and scrolling through images of attractive friends and celebrities can lead individuals (mostly girls and women, who are more likely than male-identified persons to interact with social media in this way) to report that they are not happy with their weight and/or appearance. Dissatisfaction with one's weight and body are factors that predict disordered eating and clinical eating disorder diagnoses, namely anorexia nervosa and bulimia nervosa. In a study by Hogue and Mills (2019), having young women engage on social media with an attractive female peer led to an increase in negative body image, whereas engaging with a family member did not. In another study, taking and posting selfies on social media caused women to report being more anxious, less confident, and less physically attractive compared to a control group (Mills et al., 2018). These harmful effects were even seen if these participants had the opportunity to touch up their selfies.

Physical health

Sleep: Not surprisingly, excessive technology can get in the way of getting good sleep. The blue light that is emitted from these devices can suppress the production of melatonin, our "sleepy" hormone that is released in darkness. This exposure to blue light may impact not only the amount of sleep (less!), but the quality of sleep because we may spend relatively less time in deep sleep—Stages 3 and 4, and REM sleep. Further, it is not only the physical aspect of our phones and technology that is impeding our sleep, but our associations with these devices, such as the constant reminders of online activities and content.

Lack of movement and poor posture: It has been found that excessive tech use in the form of scrolling social media or playing video games promotes a sedentary lifestyle and is associated with a host of health problems. Looking at our phones or devices for prolonged periods of time can also lead to neck pain and bad posture. That is why it is imperative to take breaks throughout the day to stretch and move our bodies. If possible, be cognizant of your posture when interacting with your technology; pull back your shoulders and stretch your neck muscles (look up!) to prevent pain and damage to your body.

Social Impact (Relationships)

Overreliance on devices has reduced the amount of time individuals are connecting with others face to face and impacted the quality of our in-person connections when they do happen. Here are a few social impacts to consider:

Early childhood development: Increasingly, parents are putting tech devices in the hands of their children. Many children are touching a device before their first birthday. Substituting technology for crucial face-to-face interactions has the potential of affecting various aspects of early childhood development, from language acquisition to basic social skills. The "social dance" that is imperative during these early years for bonding and developing a sense of safety—where caregivers and infants engage in a back-and-forth dialogue with babbling sounds, words, and expressive eye contact—may be altered and decreasing in frequency. Now, more than ever, caregivers are holding a cell phone or device while trying to communicate with their children. What will be the impact of these altered interactions, not only for children, but for the adults that have them in their care?

Reading emotional cues:[21] Spending too much time on tech devices can impact our ability to read emotions on another person's face. In a study with preteens, it was found that kids who "detoxed" at an overnight camp, where they spent five days away from technology and were encouraged to interact with their peers, showed significant improvements from their pre-test levels at reading facial expressions. These children's scores were compared to those of the control group, which showed no improvement over the five-day period (Uhls et al., 2014). Being able to read another person's emotions is integral in developing effective social skills. Getting it "right" by accurately detecting that a person is angry versus sad or anxious is an important skill for knowing how to react or respond. Getting it "wrong" can have some negative consequences in our peer relationships. For example, incorrectly reading "anger" in another person's facial expression may lead you to respond aggressively. This is not only a concern for children and teens, but adults as well. Most of what we communicate is non-verbal in nature. If our ability to correctly read these cues is slowly eroding with increasing interactions with tech devices, what are some of the potential consequences to our relationships?

Phubbing: This term refers to "phone snubbing." As a people watcher, I often notice individuals getting together for tea, coffee, or a meal, and then watch as each pulls out their phone as they are conversing with one another. What does this behaviour convey to the other person? Does it communicate that what they are saying is not that important or perhaps that they are not important enough to be given full attention? What can a string of this behaviour do to the strength of one's relationship with another person? The research to date has highlighted the detrimental effects of this behaviour, not only at a personal level (e.g., depression) but at the interpersonal level (e.g., relationship satisfaction, relationship quality). For a review of the literature, consult Al-Saggaf and O'Donnell's (2019) comprehensive article on the topic.

Miscommunication: Regardless of how we communicate, whether in-person or online via texting and emails, there is the potential for miscommunication. I am sure that we all have at least one example of a digital message that was

---

[21] Lisa Barrett-Feldman, author of *How Emotions are Made*, has been at the forefront of challenging a claim that has been accepted since Darwin. She cites research that contradicts the popular belief that emotions are universal and humans have the ability to detect them by inspecting facial expressions. In a recent interview, Feldman states, "… how people convey anger, disgust, fear, happiness, sadness, and surprise varies considerably across cultures, situations, and even across people experiencing the same incident. Barrett adds that some facial movements, such as a scowl, often communicate something other than an emotional state. People also scowl when they're confused or concentrating on something, she says" (Sarwari, 2019). Further evidence that we would be well served by remaining curious in our social interactions, and by coming back to Thich Nhất Hạnh's (1999) question, *"Are you sure?"* Her book is a fascinating read.

not perceived as intended. Perhaps you are reading an email and detecting some anger or resentment or reacting to a curt text message. Maybe you are correct, and the sender is put off in some way. *Or,* is it possible that they were in a hurry and didn't have the time to send a lengthier and more thoughtful message in between appointments? Recently, I attended a webinar with Erica Dhawan, author of *Digital Body Language,* where she tackled this issue. As the sender, can we be more mindful of how we construct the messages we send to our friends or colleagues? Our greeting, our closing remark, and the inclusion of an emoji or not can impact how our message is received by another person. With respect to the inclusion of emojis in digital messages, when sending a work-related email, think twice before adding a smiling emoji within your message. Although smiling in face-to-face contexts is associated with perceptions of warmth and competence, this is not necessarily the case in digital communications. In fact, adding a smiling face does not increase perceptions of warmth, but *decreases* perceptions of competence (Glikson et al., 2018)! Reflect on how many arguments or hurt feelings have resulted from the miscommunications described above. Consider this topic of digital body language when sending and receiving digital communications.

Cyberbullying and cancel culture: Something has changed over the years. There is a shaming/blaming/bullying element that has seeped into our public discourse. Social media has amplified this harassment and has created an environment for cruel and offensive behaviours, often shielded by a veil of anonymity. Cyberbullying can take many forms, from harassment (e.g., cruel messaging online), to exclusion (e.g., ostracizing an individual from their social group). This online bullying is also ongoing, taking place 24/7, unlike traditional bullying that ceased once away from abusers.

Cognitive Impact

Distraction: Numerous studies show that having our cell phones near us can reduce cognitive capacity. Even if our phone is off and tucked away, it is still a distraction! In a study by Ward and his colleagues (2017), university students were randomly assigned to one of three groups: the "desk" group (their phone was face down on the desk), the "pocket/bag" group (their phone was kept near them in a pocket or bag), and the "other room" group (their phone was kept outside the room). They were given various exercises to work on that tested their working memory and fluid intelligence. The results indicated that the group that performed the worst on these tests was the "desk" group, followed by the "pocket/bag" group. Even when they could not see their phone, it was still a distraction. After the study, individuals in these two groups shared that they did not believe their phones to be a distraction (they were wrong!). Their phones were tapping into their limited cognitive capacity in what the authors referred to as a "brain drain."

FIGURE 13: EFFECT OF RANDOMLY ASSIGNED PHONE LOCATION CONDITION ON AVAILABLE WORKING MEMORY CAPACITY (PANEL A) AND FLUID INTELLIGENCE (PANEL B).

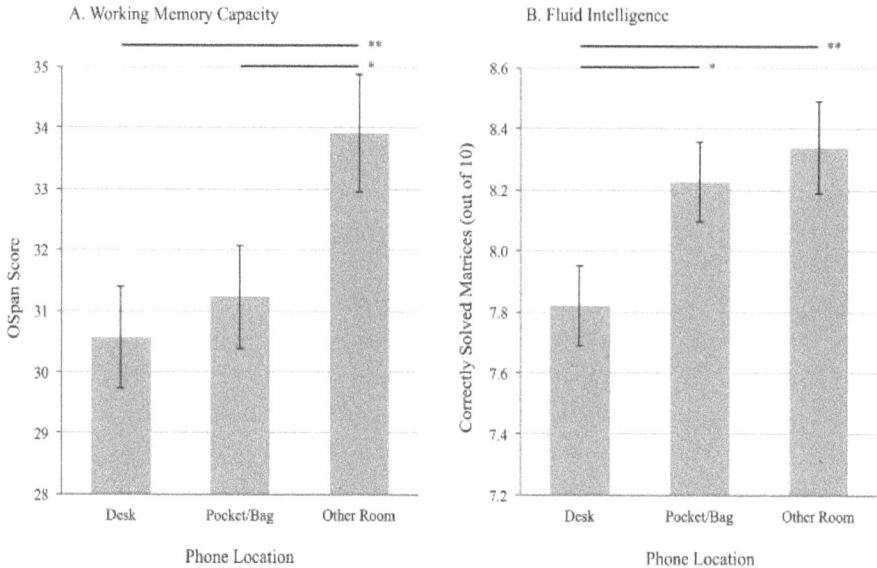

Source: Ward et al. (2017)

As you can imagine, if a powered-off, silent phone can impact your performance in this way, imagine what normally happens when your phone is on you. It is buzzing, pinging, and vibrating throughout the day. You may feel overwhelmed by this constant flow of information and notifications emanating from these devices. They are a constant reminder of what you should or could be doing instead of the task at hand. These visual, audio, and tactile stimulations (and phantom ones!) are contributing to brain drain. You may be devoting your afternoon to writing a paper or report, but are you *really* investing a few hours into this task? When we are distracted from a current task, it takes quite a bit of time to re-engage after we have been interrupted— in one study, 23 minutes and 15 seconds on average, to be exact (Gallup, 2006). By losing our focus, multiple times per day, we become less productive.

Why is it that you feel like you *need* to check your phone and email? It is because these systems have positive intermittent reinforcement inherent in their design; just like a gambler who keeps pulling the lever at the slot machine, you keep pulling the levers in these systems. You keep checking because maybe you will get an email, response, or "like" you have been waiting for. If your insistent distractibility is part of being human, what can you do to overcome these deliberate temptations? One solution is to make changes or tweaks to your working and living environments so that you can help yourself remain more focused (see *The How* section below for some tips). Remember, the "other room" group performed best in the study. Perhaps you will keep your phone in another room the next time you work on a project. And while you are at it, shut down your browser and email as well!

Polarization: One of the troublesome observations in this online age is that there is growing polarization among online users, which can lead to aggressive and harmful behaviours. Sometimes people do not hold moderate viewpoints but extreme opinions with little room for caveats and qualifications. The individuals behind creating this online information environment have purposely fed us materials that reinforce what we already believe. It shouldn't be surprising that if we are funnelled materials that advocate particular viewpoints, you see people holding an alternate viewpoint as "dumb," "naive," or "incompetent" in some way. How can they believe that? Easily! They too are consuming information that reinforces their point of view, and their initial views become more entrenched thanks to the confirmation bias not only built into these online systems but our own human psyche. We purposefully search out and consume information that *confirms* what we already believe. So where do we go from here? One strategy is to try to acknowledge and then override these inherent biases. Make a point of speaking to someone who holds a different point of view, and be curious and open to listening to what they have to say. Purposefully read newspapers and articles that advocate another point of view. I know too much about human cognition and our inherent biases to do anything else!

THE HOW

By nature, we are easily distracted. There are strategies to help us avoid digital temptations, such as increasing our mindfulness—by formally engaging in a mindfulness meditation practice, or perhaps more informally by learning to become more mindful in our conversations and daily activities. Coupled with this, we can modify our external environments so that we engage with our technology less often and in a different manner. Start by taking stock of your digital activity right now. You can check your settings and see how much you are on your cell phone each day—I bet it is more than you think! Then consider some of the following suggestions:

- *Shut off all notifications.* Yes, all of them!

- *Create some rules around your technology.* Some ideas:

  º Don't use your phone for the first and last hour of your day. You can start small (e.g., the first and last 10 minutes of the day) and work your way up.

  º Only check your email three times per day.

  º Keep your phone in another room or a locker while you attend class, meetings, or work on a project. If you are worried that you will miss an important phone call during these "do not disturb" times, you can also allow key contacts (e.g., your child's school) to come through in case of an emergency. Use the features of your devices to help you stick to your goals.

  º Consider giving up one or more social media platforms. This may be a scary prospect for you, but one that may warrant some further consideration.

  º No technology while eating and/or socializing with family and friends. Invite your company to take part in this challenge by tucking away all devices or putting them in the middle of the table. I am a proponent of the former "out of sight, out of mind" approach. You can also create a game out of it—the first person to touch their phone buys drinks or desserts for everyone around the table!

- *Take part in a digital detox.* Perhaps you will take one day during the weekend to stay away from your cell phone and/or other technology. This may be an opportunity to practice some self-care. In my Positive Psychology classes, students can choose to take part in a digital detox challenge (four hours away from all technology; if it needs a battery or to be plugged in, it is off limits!). Students then share their range of experiences, from an anguishing and nearly impossible feat to their new-found freedom as they more fully engage in activities. An increase in productivity is often a welcome by-product of this exercise. Add these regularly scheduled detox days in your calendar: or challenge yourself on these special days:

  º Digital Detox Day (DDD), beginning of September: https://www.digitaldetoxday.org

  º Global Day of Unplugging, first weekend in March (24 hours, from sundown to sundown): https://www.unplugcollaborative.org/

The goal is to create more choice. Instead of mindlessly checking and swiping, can we create a more empowering relationship with these devices? This is part of a broader goal: to be more mindful while interacting with our family and friends, more deeply engaged in solo activities (instead of scrolling through our technologies out of discomfort and/or boredom), and to live our life with more depth and substance. What this looks like for each of us will be different; reflect on the suggestions outlined above and create the conditions and environment that will promote your productivity and well-being.

WOW TIP 12:
APPLY YOUR STRENGTHS

*Everybody is a genius. But if you judge a fish by its ability
to climb a tree, it will live its whole life believing it is stupid.*

~ Albert Einstein

THE WHAT

When the science of positive psychology began to explode in the early 2000s, one key topic emerged: *character strengths*. In 2004, Christopher Peterson and Martin Seligman wrote the seminal book *Character Strengths and Virtues*. According to the VIA Institute on Character website (https://www. viacharacter.org), a site devoted to this topic, character strengths are "the positive parts of [our] personality that impact how [we] think, feel and behave" (VIA Institute on Character, n.d.). They identified 24 character strengths, clustered under six virtue categories (as shown in Table 4). Each of us has a unique character strengths profile, as we possess all 24 strengths in varying degrees. To take the free test, see *The How* section below.

TABLE 4: LIST OF 24 CHARACTER STRENGTHS

WISDOM (HEAD STRENGTHS)	COURAGE (HEART STRENGTHS)	HUMANITY (STRENGTH OF OTHERS)
• Creativity • Curiosity • Love of Learning • Judgment • Perspective	• Bravery • Perseverance • Honesty • Zest	• Love • Kindness • Social Intelligence
TEMPERANCE (SELF STRENGTHS)	**JUSTICE (COMMUNITY STRENGTHS)**	**TRANSCENDENCE (STRENGTH OF SPIRIT)**
• Forgiveness • Humility • Prudence • Self-Regulation	• Fairness • Leadership • Teamwork	• Appreciation of Beauty/Excellence • Gratitude • Humour • Spirituality • Hope

Source: Adapted from Peterson & Seligman (2004)

THE WHY

In an early study by Seligman and his colleagues (2005), it was demonstrated that using one's signature strengths in a new and unique way is an effective intervention for increasing happiness and decreasing depression for six months. Several other studies have shown that strengths-based interventions can improve well-being. As highlighted on the sign-on page for the assessment, knowing and using your character strengths can help you increase your happiness and well-being, find meaning and happiness, boost your relationships, manage stress, be healthier, and accomplish your goals. For an in-depth summary of studies, visit the VIA Institute on Character website: https://www.viacharacter.org/research/findings.

THE HOW

To take the free Values in Action (VIA) strengths survey of 24 strengths (it should take you approximately 15 minutes to complete), follow this link: https://www.viacharacter.org/survey/account/register. You also have the option to pay a nominal fee to receive a VIA report, an in-depth analysis of your unique strengths profile.

MY TOP 5 VIA STRENGTHS

1. _____

2. _____

3. _____

4. _____

5. _____

Additional thoughts/observations:

Using One of My Top Strengths in a Novel Way

Reflect on your results. Then challenge yourself: Can you use at least one of your top strengths in a novel way?

Reflect on your "weaknesses" or your "lesser strengths" (this latter phrase reflects a strengths-based perspective). Peterson, before his unexpected passing in 2012, was working on a theory on how psychological disorders could be reconceptualized by viewing them as the opposite, absence, or excess of strengths. Although unfinished, he left the following chart (Table 5) as an alternative to the *Diagnostic and Statistical Manual*, 5th edition (DSM-5), our current system of classifying mental illnesses in North America.[22]

---

[22] More recently, Ryan Niemiec, Education Director of the VIA Institute, has further developed this idea in his recent article "Finding the golden mean: The overuse, underuse, and optimal use of character strengths" (2019).

TABLE 5: THE 72 "PETERSON PATHOLOGIES"

VIRTUE	STRENGTH	OPPOSITE	ABSENCE	EXCESS
Wisdom	Creativity	Triteness	Conformity	Eccentricity
	Curiosity	Boredom	Disinterest	Nosiness
	Love of learning	Gullibility	Ineffectiveness	Cynicism
	Judgment	Orthodoxy	Complacency	Know-it-all-ism
	Perspective	Foolishness	Shallowness	Ivory tower
Courage	Bravery	Cowardice	Fright	Foolhardiness
	Perseverance	Helplessness	Laziness	Obsessiveness
	Honesty	Deceit	Phoniness	Righteousness
	Zest	Lifelessness	Restraint	Hyperactivity
Humanity (Love)	Love	Loneliness	Isolation/autism	Emotional promiscuity
	Kindness	Cruelty	Indifference	Intrusiveness
	Social intelligence	Self-destruction	Obtuseness	Psycho-babbling
Justice	Teamwork	Narcissism	Selfishness	Chauvinism
	Fairness	Prejudice	Partisanship	Detachment
	Leadership	Sabotage	Compliance	Despotism
Temperance (Moderation)	Forgiveness	Vengefulness	Mercilessness	Permissiveness
	Humility	Arrogance	Footless self-esteem	Self-deprecation
	Prudence	Recklessness	Sensation-seeking	Prudishness
	Self-regulation	Impulsivity	Self-indulgence	Inhibition
Transcendence	Appreciation of beauty & excellence	Criticism	Oblivion	Snobbery
	Gratitude	Entitlement	Rudeness	Ingratiation
	Hope	Despair	Present orientation	Pollyannaism
	Humour	Dourness	Humour-lessness	Buffoonery
	Spirituality	Alienation	Anomie	Fanaticism

Source: Adapted from Seligman (2015)

As an alternative to the VIA strengths survey, Gallup has created the CliftonStrengths survey of 34 strengths. To learn more about this assessment tool (Note: It is not free), visit: https://www.gallup.com/cliftonstrengths. This survey was developed with the workplace in mind. In comparison, the orientation of the VIA survey is broader in scope, as the 24 strengths identified are universal, and this tool is not setting/situation specific.

WOW TIPS: BEYOND ME

The WOW tips we have discussed thus far have all focused on the individual ("me"). This last category, Beyond Me, focuses on three main strategies:

- WOW Tip 13: Discover and Live Your Purpose

- WOW Tip 14: Foster Connection

- WOW Tip 15: Help Others

The topic of purpose could have been organized under the "Mind" strategies (see *WOW Tip 7: Make Meaning as You Create Empowering Stories*). But I have decided to categorize it here, as one's sense of purpose often contains an other-focused orientation, with an aim beyond the individual. The second strategy, fostering connection, is integral to well-being and happiness. The research shows that a person's sense of well-being is linked to being well-connected with others, even if it is just one person or a select few. Finally, the power of helping others; I will share with you a wealth of research that shows that even a small gesture to help others can benefit not only the recipient, but us too.

WOW TIP 13:
DISCOVER AND LIVE
YOUR PURPOSE

The two most important days in your life are
the day you are born and the day you find out why.

~ Mark Twain

He who has a why to live,
can bear almost any how.

~ Friedrich Nietzsche

THE WHAT

Purpose refers to the direction in which you want to move. According to Kashdan and McKnight (2009), purpose is our "central, self-organizing life aim" that generates continual goals and targets. It is not a list of goals; if you can check it off a to-do list, it is a goal, *not* your purpose. But your goals are related to your purpose. For example, if you want to be a social worker, that is a goal. *What kind* of social worker you want to be speaks to purpose—what impact do you want to have on the people you work with? What *kind of* parent do you want to be, and what impact do you want to have on your children? One suggestion is to think about purpose as a verb expressing movement toward goals that are often bigger than us.

Related to this topic is the concept of job crafting—creating meaning and purpose in our paid and unpaid work (Berg et al., 2008). If you are employed, ask yourself: *Why* do you do what you do? Is it for a paycheque (thus, a job) or are you serving a bigger purpose (a calling)? For an in-depth analysis of this topic, see *WOW Tip 7: Make Meaning as You Create Empowering Stories.*

THE WHY

According to McKnight and Kashdan (2009), purpose leads to living a longer life, a lower likelihood of health problems, and a higher satisfaction with one's life. Vic Strecher reinforces these findings in his book *Life on Purpose* and in his TED Talks *On Purpose* and *Life on Purpose*. He highlights that living a purposeful life is associated with a lowered risk of heart disease, stroke, and Alzheimer's disease, less stress, and better sleep at night, among other benefits (Strecher, 2016).

THE HOW

Step 1: Discover your values—what is important to you?

1. Values Questionnaire

Reflect on the following valued domains and identify which ones are most important to you. Then, for each item ask yourself how closely your behaviours are aligned with your values (see the next page for a list of core values). The more closely you align with your values, the higher your general sense of well-being. When you feel distress, come back to what matters most to you.

QUESTIONNAIRE 2: VALUES QUESTIONNAIRE (ADAPTATION OF THE VLQ[23])

VALUED DOMAIN	IMPORTANCE[*]	ALIGNMENT[†]
Family		
Marriage/Couples/Intimate Relations		
Parenting		
Friends/Social Life		
Work		
Education/Training		
Recreation/Fun		
Spirituality		
Community Life		
Physical Self-Care (e.g., diet, exercise, sleep)		

* 1: low importance
  10: high importance

† 1: behaviours not at all aligned with my values
  10: behaviours completely aligned with my values

---

[23] The Valued Living Questionnaire (VLQ) was created by Kelly Wilson and later adapted by Russ Harris, author of *The Happiness Trap* and expert in Acceptance and Commitment Therapy (ACT). The table here is an adaptation of his Values Worksheet tool. To explore this adapted tool, see Harris (2008) under References.

2. Core Values Checklist (Harris, 2010)

Which of the following values are most important to you at this point in your life?

☐ Acceptance	☐ Flexibility	☐ Persistence
☐ Adventure	☐ Freedom	☐ Pleasure
☐ Assertiveness	☐ Friendliness	☐ Power
☐ Authenticity	☐ Forgiveness	☐ Reciprocity
☐ Beauty	☐ Fun	☐ Respect
☐ Caring	☐ Generosity	☐ Responsibility
☐ Challenge	☐ Gratitude	☐ Romance
☐ Compassion	☐ Honesty	☐ Safety
☐ Connection	☐ Humour	☐ Self-awareness
☐ Contribution	☐ Humility	☐ Self-care
☐ Conformity	☐ Industry	☐ Self-development
☐ Cooperation	☐ Independence	☐ Self-control
☐ Courage	☐ Intimacy	☐ Sensuality
☐ Creativity	☐ Justice	☐ Sexuality
☐ Curiosity	☐ Kindness	☐ Spirituality
☐ Encouragement	☐ Love	☐ Skilfulness
☐ Equality	☐ Mindfulness	☐ Supportiveness
☐ Excitement	☐ Order	☐ Trust
☐ Fairness	☐ Open-mindedness	☐ _____
☐ Fitness	☐ Patience	☐ _____

List your top 5 values here:

1. _____
2. _____
3. _____
4. _____
5. _____

3. Peak Life Experience

Take a moment to think back over your life so far. Identify a Peak Life Experience. This is a moment that has personal significance for you. You might have felt fully energized, absorbed, and alive, and/or experienced a sense of joy, awe, pride, or accomplishment. Describe this experience in as much detail as possible.

4. Best Possible Self Exercise

Imagine your life in the future. What is the best possible life you can imagine? Consider all the relevant areas, such as your career, academic work, relationships, hobbies, personal and spiritual growth, and/or health. What would happen in these areas of your life in your best possible future?

5. Six Months to Live Exercise

Sometimes you need to feel a bit of pressure to figure out what you want. Imagine for a moment that you only have six months left to live. This means that you've got nothing to lose, and you are not fearful of failing or trying something new. What would you do? What would you want to learn? Where would you want to go? Who would you like to be with?

6. Tombstone Exercise

Spend some time thinking about what you would want written on your tombstone. What do you want to be remembered for? What would your legacy be? What would you want people to say about you at your memorial service?

Reflect on how you responded to these six exercises. What came up for you? As you reflect on your life at this moment, are you aligning with what matters most to you? Did you highlight that your family and friends are something that you highly value, but much of your time and energy is spent on work that often excludes these individuals? Confronting one's death as you did with the Six Months to Live Exercise and the Tombstone Exercise can be uncomfortable tasks to complete, but they can shake us into reprioritizing what is in front of us. BJ Miller, a palliative care doctor with a touching TED Talk entitled *What Really Matters at the End of Life*, summed it up in a short video he did for PBS's *Brief but Spectacular* series: "There's this side effect that seems to come by facing mortality: It seems to inform how you live. So, the secret is that facing death has a lot to do with living well." He should know. As a university student, he sustained an almost fatal accident and lost both legs and part of his right arm when he was out one night with friends. He reflected on this experience and shared that "some way life is not going to do what you want it to do … you will suffer. It is unavoidable. Then there's this unnecessary rind of suffering which is so—which is the demoralizing part because it's the invented stuff. It comes in terms of how we treat each other, sometimes poorly. It comes in those moments of abandonment" (PBS, 2016). He reminds us of our humanity; we all suffer and struggle. For me, the problem is not that we have these experiences, but our attachments to these events, these emotions, the "invented stuff"—the unnecessary layer we add to our experiences (recall the second arrow!). In these times, can we survive the challenges and possible traumas we experience, not despite them, but *because of* them?

Step 2: Discover your purpose (or "ikigai")

My hope for you is that along the way, you will discover your *ikigai*, a Japanese word meaning "a reason for being." This is our purpose. So how do we get to purpose? According to Kashdan and McKnight (2009), there are three pathways:

1. *Proactive:* This involves putting in gradual effort over time with a curious mind and a willingness to explore new experiences. One discovers their purpose after refinement and clarification. If you have started to complete the exercises on pages 128–133 and you are committed to reflecting deeply on your responses, you are partaking in this pathway.

2. *Reactive:* This pathway is not one that you choose to encounter, but one that is thrust upon you. It involves discovering your purpose after experiencing a transformative event (e.g., trauma, near-death

experience). These events force individuals to re-evaluate, introspect, seek out rewarding behaviours, and make meaning (Bonanno, 2004). Revisit *WOW Tip 7: Make Meaning as You Create Empowering Stories* to review the concept of post-traumatic growth and ways we can make meaning of our experiences.

3. *Social Learning:* This pathway involves discovering one's purpose via observation, imitation, and modelling.

My Purpose Statement

Please write your purpose statement here. Remember, it is not a list of things to do; it is about the direction in which you want to move. It can be relatively narrow and brief (i.e., one sentence) or broader and/or lengthier. Short purpose statements are narrowly focused and clearly highlight the aim (e.g., "I live to create the best-tasting cupcakes in Hamilton ... or the world!"). You choose your scope. Others are more broadly focused. I will share mine with you here:

> *To inspire those around me to live a full life ... with accomplishments and failures, gains and losses, love and hurt ... whole-heartedly, authentically and with compassion. To appreciate what we have, with gratitude. To cultivate my relationships with family and friends ... despite challenges, to seek comfort in knowing that we have each other's backs. To be mindful and remain curious, free from judgment.*

WOW TIP 14:
FOSTER CONNECTION

Other people matter.

~ Christopher Peterson

*I define connection as the energy that exists between
people when they feel seen, heard, and valued; when
they can give and receive without judgment; and when
they derive sustenance and strength from the relationship.*

~ Brené Brown

THE WHAT & WHY

Ubuntu

One word that I want to highlight here as we begin our discussion is the African word *ubuntu*. In simple terms, it is captured in these words: "I am because *we* are." Vivek Murthy, author of *Together* (2020), writes, "There's a special phrase in Zulu—'Umuntu ngumuntu ngabantu,' which means 'I am because you are, and you are because we are.' This ideal is instilled in the term 'ubuntu,' meaning to live through others … ubuntu stresses one's connection to the group first, and harmony foremost." Notable figures have referenced this concept. For example, during an anti-apartheid campaign in the 1980s, Desmond Tutu stated:

> One of the sayings in our country is ubuntu—the essence of being human. Ubuntu speaks particularly about the fact that you can't exist as a human being in isolation. It speaks about our interconnectedness. You can't be human all by yourself, and when you have this quality—ubuntu—you are known for your generosity. We think of ourselves far too frequently as just individuals, separated from one another, whereas you are connected and what you do affects the whole world. When you do well, it spreads out; it is for the whole of humanity (as cited in Tuleja, 2022).

Nelson Mandela, Barack Obama, Bill Clinton, and Doc Rivers are others that have popularized the term. In the 2000s, Doc Rivers introduced ubuntu to the Boston Celtics basketball team, in his role as head coach. Coincidentally, they won the NBA championship in 2008, in what I would like to believe is in part because of the power of ubuntu. To deepen your understanding of this concept, you may want to explore the Mnyaka and Motlhabi (2005) paper on the subject. According to these authors:

> Although there is no single definition of ubuntu, all the definitions cited imply that ubuntu is more than just a manifestation of individual acts. Rather, it is a spiritual foundation, an inner state, an orientation, and a good disposition that motivates, challenges and makes one perceive, feel and act in a humane way towards others. It is a way of life that seeks to promote and manifest itself and is best realized or evident in harmonious relations in society.

The Importance of Human Connection

We are social animals and have evolved to belong to groups. In their book, *The Good Life* (2023), Robert Waldinger, the director of the Harvard Study of Adult Development, and his co-author, Marc Schulz, found that strong personal connections were the most powerful predictor of overall happiness and better health, trumping money, fame, IQ, and other factors. This message is repeatedly highlighted in their book, and in Waldinger's (2015) TED Talk entitled *What Makes a Good Life?*, in which he states, "Good relationships keep us happier and healthier. Period." The Harvard study, one of the most famous longitudinal studies ever conducted, recruited 724 boys and men in 1938 (of these participants, 268 were white male sophomores; the remaining 456 were inner-city Boston boys). Since then, they have expanded their research pool and are now tracking three generations and more than 1,300 of the original cohort's descendants. Over 80 years of extensive research, the conclusion is always the same: Human connection matters! Their reference to connection not only includes our relationships to our family and friends, but also our communities. I encourage you to take a moment to learn more about this study, and the importance of human connection to our well-being.

Defining the Problem … Disconnection and Loneliness

One way to highlight the pivotal role of connection and belongingness to well-being is to observe what happens when there is a lack of these connections. Over time, we are becoming more disconnected from essential social networks. Many experts have commented that we are the loneliest generation ever, and there is evidence that it is impacting not only our mental health, with increasing rates of depression, but our physical health as well. A 2006 American survey reported a tripling of the number of people who admitted that they did not have a single person with whom to discuss important matters. In fact, these individuals without a single confidant made up almost one out of four people surveyed—the *modal* number, the most popular response (McPherson et al., 2006). Although this study was published in 2006, these trends are continuing today and can be seen on our side of the border as well. In a recent Angus Reid survey (2019), over 60% of Canadians reported that they would like their family and friends to spend more time with them. One-third reported that they could not definitely say that they could rely on family or friends to provide financial support if needed, and almost 20% were not sure if they could count on another for emotional support during a crisis. These rates are alarming, but perhaps they should not be surprising. We may have the false impression that it is the quantity of our social connections that matters, and having hundreds of "friends" on social media may give us this idea that we are well-connected. It isn't the number of connections, but the quality of these relationships that matters. Another distinction is the difference between social isolation and loneliness. One can be in a crowded room and feel utterly lonely, or alone and feel well-connected. Loneliness refers to our relative satisfaction with the quality of our social connections (a subjective feeling), whereas social isolation is the number and frequency of these connections (an objective measure). Although these are distinct constructs, there is a relationship between them; Canadians who live alone report higher levels of loneliness versus those who live with others. This is a concern, because one-person households have steadily increased over the decades, increasing from 7% in 1951 to 28% in 2016 (Statistics Canada, 2017). Social isolation is also compounded by lack of community engagement, including visiting neighbours, volunteering, and attending events. Loneliness is highest among young women, indicated by findings that approximately 60% of women aged 18–34 sometimes or often wish they had someone to talk to, but don't (Angus Reid, 2019). They were also much more likely to *feel* alone, even when with other people.

Consequences of Disconnection and Loneliness

Connection is why we're here.
We are hardwired to connect with others,
it's what gives purpose and meaning
to our lives, and without it there is suffering.

~ Brené Brown

Recall from our introductory positive psychology chapter the "I" in illness and "we" in wellness. One of the consequences of this disconnection is that social isolation hurts. Literally. There is research (Eisenberger et al., 2003, and

Kross et al., 2011, as cited in Fogel, 2012) to suggest that the pain centres of the brain, the anterior insula and the anterior cingulate cortex, are activated when we are hurt, regardless of the source of that pain. In other words, if we are isolated or ostracized from a social group (emotional pain) or if we fall and consequently hurt ourselves (physical pain), the same pain centres in our brains light up.

In addition to this connection with pain, Murthy (2020) highlights the mounting evidence that loneliness is related to poorer mental and physical health, including increased rates of heart disease, stroke, dementia, depression, and anxiety. The late John Cacioppo, a loneliness expert, has echoed these findings in countless articles and in his 2013 TED Talk, *The Lethality of Loneliness*. Johann Hari, author of *Lost Connections* (2019), interviewed Cacioppo extensively, and highlights the link between loneliness and depression. Hari points out that loneliness is often a causal agent in depression. And unfortunately, many of the remedies that we offer individuals (i.e., medications and other treatments) do not address one of the root causes of their depression: loneliness. In no way am I suggesting that there is a simplistic explanation for depression in that it is only about loneliness. The research supports the idea that multiple factors (including biological and social ones) interact to explain one's mental health, and epigenetics offers an explanation about how these factors may interact.

THE HOW

How can we develop deep and meaningful connections in our lives? The first step is to make the time to connect with others. Then, when we are connecting, we should be mindful about how we are showing up in these interactions. Below are some tips.

Tip 1: Communicate, Communicate, Communicate

Regardless of whether we are talking about our relationships with family, friends, co-workers, or an intimate partner, open and honest communication is key. Communication is a two-way process, involving what we are saying with our words and our bodies *and* how we are listening to and receiving the messages of others. If you are communicating via technology on your phone or via Zoom, are you paying attention to the conversation, or are you phubbing ("phone snubbing") the other person? Take this opportunity to practice mindfulness.

If you find yourself without family and/or friends with whom to connect, then finding and making friendships is where you will need to start. You are not alone; remember, a significant number of people (one in four) do not have a single person with whom to discuss important matters. So, where can we start looking? One option is to start in your community. What are your interests? If you like reading, you can visit the local library and join a book club. If you like to walk or run, visit your local community centre or contact a running store and join a group. If you have creative interests such as painting or pottery, sign up for a class at your local community centre, art centre, or college. Look at volunteer opportunities in your community; by sharing your talents and/or time, maybe your strengths can benefit others. There are online forums and groups as well, especially if meeting others in person is intimidating for you. If you feel that social anxiety is holding you back from making these connections, speak to a healthcare professional to receive additional support. Addressing an underlying fear or concern and building these vital social skills can help you gain confidence so that you can meet people.

Two individuals that have done extensive research in the area of flourishing relationships are the powerhouse duo John Gottman and his partner Julie Schwartz Gottman. Their work has primarily focused on intimate relationships, but their advice is generalizable across all relationships. According to John Gottman, in his book *The Seven Principles for Making Marriage Work* (2000), co-authored with Nan Silver, couples often make numerous mistakes that increase their chances of ending up in an unhappy partnership or heading toward divorce. In fact, Gottman can observe a couple discussing a contentious issue for as little as five minutes and determine with 91% accuracy whether they will divorce. What is he looking at? The six factors include: harsh start-ups, the four horsemen of the apocalypse (criticism, contempt, defensiveness, and stonewalling), flooding, body language, failed repair attempts, and bad memories (Gottman & Silver, 2000). Think about what you may be communicating to your partner, family member, friend, or co-worker when you engage in some of these practices. Are you conveying respect? One of the worst things you can do when communicating with another person, with your words *and* body language, is to express contempt for them. Contempt is attacking a person's character by insulting or demeaning them in some way or conveying disgust for them (e.g., by rolling your eyes or sighing when they speak). There will be times when we will disagree with the people in our lives. But how do we express our frustration without hurting the other person's feelings? Here are some tips to keep in mind:

- *Ground yourself.* Before engaging in a difficult conversation, check in with yourself. Do you need to calm down? Can you benefit from taking a few deep breaths, or engaging in another activity that can ground you in this moment?

- *Engage in some perspective-taking.* Be curious. Can you see the situation from the other person's perspective? Reframe your current interaction. If you are coming into this discussion with a "I will win" or "I am right and you are wrong" mentality, you are setting yourself up for failure. Observing the situation from a me-versus-you lens and keeping score by tallying the other person's misdoings are signs that you are not in this together. Challenge your perspective and view it with a "we lens": *We* are in this together with the goal of moving in the same direction.

- *Use "I-statements."* Gordon Thomas introduced this concept in the 1960s as a form of communication that is less likely to be critical to the listener (Gottman & Silver, 2000). For example, "I am angry/ frustrated/upset *because* the garbage wasn't taken out" shifts the focus to your emotional experience. There is no need to blame the other person and point your finger by using "*you*" language: "*You* meant to hurt me," "*You* did this on purpose," or "*You* are lazy." Although it can be challenging at times, we should do our best to disentangle the action from the person, and refrain from making a dispositional attribution, inferring something about the *kind of person* they are. Can you be certain that the behaviour was intentional? Is it fair to characterize your partner or roommate as lazy, or is this an opportunity for some much-needed perspective taking? Are they lazy, or are they simply overwhelmed/overworked/distracted with a personal issue and need some downtime? (Remember, we need free space in our calendars!) In contrast, when you use "I-statements" the other person cannot argue with what you are sharing with them. You *own* your emotional experience; they cannot say that you do not feel angry/frustrated/ upset. By being specific, you are connecting your emotional experience to a specific event.

- *Avoid saying "You always" or "You never."* You know you are entering minefield territory when you use absolute language. If your partner, family member, friend, or co-worker ever engaged in a behaviour contrary to your accusation, just one time, you are incorrect. Busted!

- *Pay attention to your body language.* Our anger/frustration/disappointment often slips through our filters via our behaviours. When you are interacting with another person, are you turning toward them or away from them? Are you "open" to a discussion, or not (e.g., crossed arms, tense shoulders)? Are you conveying signs of contempt by rolling your eyes or sneering at them? Expressing your superiority with your words or actions is one of the most dangerous things you can do in a relationship.

Tip 2: Lean into Vulnerability

In Brené Brown's best-selling book *Daring Greatly* (2012a), *vulnerability* involves "uncertainty, risk, and emotional exposure." Vulnerability can be uncomfortable, Brown asserts, because it involves taking risks, sharing our stories, and confronting the possibility that we may not be accepted and/or loved in return. But repeated experiences of empathy—feeling with people— and validation—knowing it's okay to feel what we are feeling—can create a space for us to be truly seen in our relationships. In her 2012 TED Talk, *Listening to Shame*, Brown asserts that vulnerability is not only vital for true human connection, but it is the "birthplace of innovation, creativity, and change" (Brown, 2012b). When we think about the people in our lives that we trust and that have our backs, who are these individuals? How do we show up to them and vice versa? At the core, they are those individuals to whom we can reveal our true selves, as imperfect as we are, and know that we will be accepted. That is true connection.

Tip 3: Convey Empathy and Validation

We cannot talk about vulnerability without highlighting the importance of empathy and validation. *Empathy* is feeling with people (Brown, 2013). According to Brown (2012a), you don't need to have experienced the situation (e.g., a job loss or break up) to feel empathy. You just need to connect with the emotion; this involves vulnerability—digging deep within yourself and connecting with the emotion this person is experiencing (Brown, 2013). Can you step outside of yourself and take on someone else's perspective by seeing and feeling their world, without judgment? Simply acknowledge that you sense/see/hear/feel that they are upset/angry/shamed. *Validation* is accepting another person's experience, including their thoughts, emotions, and behaviours, regardless of whether you agree with or approve of them (Hall, 2012). It has the power of lessening the intensity of your emotional response and strengthening your relationships with others. Having another person validate your experience (e.g., by saying "That must be hard," or "That sucks, what happened to you") communicates that it is okay to feel what you are feeling, without judgment. Think about this response in comparison to invalidating responses: "It is not really that bad," "It could have been worse," and "At least you still have your relationship/job/health."

Brown (2013) warns us that empathetic responses rarely, if ever, start with "At least you …." If you find yourself starting your sentence in this way, stop right there. Invalidating someone's struggle with a statement like this can do more harm. It is natural for many of us to want to swoop in, fix, and minimize a person's pain. But some of these attempts, while well-intentioned, can backfire. A comforting statement is sometimes all that your partner, family member, friend, or co-worker needs to hear, at least for right now. At other times, there can be great comfort in the power of silence. I think that many of us can agree that we feel uncomfortable when no one is talking, and we often speak just to fill in this space. But sometimes, silence is exactly what is needed. I recently listened to a talk that introduced me to this acronym of WAIT: *Why Am I Talking?* Can you benefit from asking yourself this question from time to time? A gentle touch on the hand or shoulder, with consent, can convey more than any words.

Tip 4: Do and Say Nice Things

Many of us think that healthy, satisfying relationships are about doing "big" things for the other person, like a grand display of affection or organizing a weekend away. Although these can be lovely ways to show someone that you care, the ordinary day-to-day signs of affection are more important. Clearing the snow off your partner's or neighbour's car. Emptying the dishwasher. Writing a sweet message on a sticky note and attaching it to your family member's computer screen. Many of these small gestures do not cost anything and often do not take much time at all, but they accumulate to show the other person how much you care.

Tip 5: Express Appreciation and Gratitude

Before you can be grateful and reap its benefits (for both of you!) for something another person said or did, you need to practice some mindfulness and notice. Acknowledging and then expressing your appreciation for something that they said or did is powerful. Be specific when expressing gratitude. Move beyond "I am grateful for you. You are just awesome!" to "I am grateful that you helped me with _____ because _____."

Tip 6: Celebrate Good News

What do you think: Is it more important how we respond to another person's good news (e.g., a promotion at work) *or* their bad news (e.g., receiving negative feedback on a work project)? Although we need to be mindful about how we respond to someone's bad news, some research has shown that it is even more important how we respond to their positive news.

Imagine the following scenario. Your partner comes home and tells you that they have been offered a promotion. Should you say:

A. "Oh, I see. I think that would mean a lot more daily stress. I don't think I would want that kind of promotion!" (active destructive)

B. "That's nice. Can you help me set the table for dinner?" (passive constructive)

C. "Oh, okay. Let me tell you what happened to me today!" (passive destructive)

D. "That is absolutely amazing news! I want to hear all about it!" (active constructive)

According to research by Gable and her colleagues (2006), an active constructive response is optimal. By putting the spotlight on them and letting them re-experience the positive emotions that are associated with this good news, you are creating an upward spiral of positivity, a reference to Fredrickson's (2004) broaden-and-build theory. When responding, consider open-ended questions so that they can share their story with you, instead of closed-ended queries that elicit yes/no answers and tend to cut the conversation short.

Tip 7: Adopt a Growth Mindset

> *When asked how they managed to stay together for 65 years,*
> *the woman replied, 'We were born in a time when if*
> *something was broke, you fixed it … not throw it away.'*

~ Author unknown

Think about your relationships with others as a work in progress. Sometimes your partner, family member, friend, or co-worker may do or say something that is hurtful; and likewise, you will not act optimally at times as well. Most of the time, it is not a sign that you should break ties or move on.[24]

---

[24] In no way am I suggesting that you should stay and work on a relationship if you feel that you are being exploited or abused in some way (i.e., physical, emotional, sexual, financial, and/or other forms of abuse). Your physical and psychological health and safety should be your top priority and your best course of action would be to sever ties and end an abusive relationship.

Instead, these transgressions are evidence that we are imperfect human beings that will make mistakes. What ideals do you have for your relationships with others? When it comes to your intimate partnerships, have you romanticized what a relationship *should* look like, having been influenced by the stories we have consumed through movies, shows, and books? And what about the other relationships in your lives? What should they look like? When it comes to evaluating your actions and those of others, you need to acknowledge that the circumstances we find ourselves in (e.g., stress, fatigue, poverty, oppression, discrimination) can impact the way we show up in the world. I know this to be true; I don't even want to be around me when I am sleep-deprived or overwhelmed with stress! Knowing first-hand the impact of not being well resourced and operating from an empty tank, I try to give those around me the benefit of the doubt. To make space. To let something go as I pick my battles; at the end, does it really matter? Are we doing the best we can with what we have? Can we work toward making it better, together?

WOW TIP 15:
HELP OTHERS

*The best way to find yourself is to lose
yourself in the service of others.*

~ Mahatma Gandhi

*We make a living by what we get,
but we make a life by what we give.*

~ Winston Churchill

THE WHAT

We are social animals and need to belong to groups. But what is our role within these networks with family, friends, and colleagues? Ideally, we will benefit from a relationship based in reciprocity, where we give and receive in our social interactions. This WOW tip will concentrate on the "giving" aspect, as there are benefits for both the giver and receiver, and for others that witness these benevolent actions. When we talk about helping others, we can offer our time, money, or other resources. Sometimes we are compensated for our actions, as we are employed in "helping" professions. Or we volunteer our time with an organization, or perhaps we care for an elderly parent or family member. These actions could be a one-time occurrence such as a random act of kindness (e.g., helping someone carry their groceries) or a longer-term commitment. Whatever we choose to do, focusing our attention outside of ourselves will serve us well.

THE WHY

There appear to be several personal and broader benefits for these altruistic actions. Here we concentrate on the benefits associated with volunteering our time.

Personal Benefits

In a recent article, Lawton and his colleagues (2020) explored the relationship between volunteering and subjective well-being (SWB). Reviewing some of the previous research, they reported that a positive correlation is often found between volunteering and various factors associated with SWB/happiness/life satisfaction. The more time spent volunteering, the higher the scores on these happiness-related variables. Is it that volunteering leads one to become happier (or less unhappy), or is it that individuals who are already happier are more likely to volunteer? Or other variables could be involved that are related to both volunteering and happiness, such as better health. Some research suggests that volunteering has greater benefits for those that are relatively unhappy as it tends to decrease unhappiness more so than it increases happiness. To try to answer this question about the directional relationship between these variables, Lawton and his colleagues (2020) used advanced statistical analyses (the details of their analyses are beyond the scope of this book). Although it was noted that, in general, happier individuals are more likely to volunteer their time, there appears to be a boost in their initial reports of happiness that results from their volunteering efforts. The paper also noted that volunteering was associated with higher well-being for those aged 16–24 and 55–74 and for individuals from both high- and low-income brackets. Regardless of one's motivation to volunteer, there appear to be advantages for helping others. Although the focus of this paper was on the relationship between volunteering and well-being, other studies have found personal benefits in terms of physical and mental health, our sense of meaning and purpose, and social connection. Several studies have demonstrated a reduction in depressive symptoms that results from helping others. Focusing on something outside of ourselves, by moving our attention away from the self and our perceived problems, can lead to a boost in our mood and well-being.

Broader Benefits Beyond the Giver

Of course, there are benefits of being the receiver of these benevolent actions. But is it possible that a contagion effect is associated with these behaviours? Yes! According to a recent meta-analysis (Jung et al., 2020, as cited in University of Texas at Austin, 2020), witnessing helpful behaviours and acts of kindness motivates us to engage in prosocial actions. Small actions can create ripple effects of goodwill.

THE HOW

There are many ways that you can help others. You can volunteer your time or engage in random acts of kindness. You may also want to donate funds if you have the financial means. Grab a friend and do something together that will benefit others. It is up to you to decide what this will look like in your life.

You may pursue a line of work where helping is central to what you do, as you directly assist others. But I would challenge you to think of a job where "helping others" is not a feature of the work. Even if you are not directly working with people, are you contributing to the greater good in some way (e.g., driving a truck of fresh fruit to a local grocery store, making a particular product in a factory)? You likely play a part in a long chain that benefits others. Think about what you do that may make someone else's life better, even in some small way.

One last caveat: If you are spending a good deal of time in a caregiving role, you need to make sure that you are taking care of yourself. You know the analogy: If there is an emergency on an aircraft, you put your oxygen mask on first before you secure one on a more vulnerable individual, such as your child or an elderly person near you. If you do not take care of yourself, no one else will be helped. See *WOW Tip 4: Practice Self-Care* for further details and suggestions.

PART III:
MOVING FROM KNOWING TO DOING—THE SCIENCE OF GOAL SETTING AND ACHIEVING

In this final chapter, we will focus on strategies that will make achieving our goals a reality. The issue is often not in the *knowing;* the struggle is in the *doing.* Many times, we have great intentions, and our "tomorrows" or "one days" look bright. But right now, we are too tired, busy, or overwhelmed to start. How do we start making our "tomorrows" a reality? We will explore evidence-based strategies that will help move us from *knowing* to *doing.*

1. *Setting goals:* How we frame our goals (and sub-goals) is important.

2. *Creating habits:* How we prepare can mean not having to exert extra energy, a limited resource!

What you will learn is that what may first appear to be a "person" problem (e.g., I suck! I am weak!) when we struggle is often a "process" problem. Do the work beforehand, make small tweaks, and reap the benefits when you realize that you are *doing* it!

SETTING GOALS (& SUB-GOALS)

Start by choosing a goal. Be thoughtful about how you state it, and pick a challenging goal. If you believe you can achieve your goal with little effort, you have not set it high enough. When possible, set an *approach* goal. It is easier to move toward something than away from it. For example, instead of framing your goal as "*not* sitting in front of the TV and watching Netflix," reframe it as "walking 10,000 steps each day."

For example:

- **My goal is to** increase my daily steps to 10,000 **by** March 1, 20__ **by** intentionally parking further away and walking with a friend on my lunch and after dinner.

- **My goal is to** declutter my home **by** May 1, 20__ **by** spending 4 hours per weekend organizing and decluttering each room in my home.

Try it!

My goal is to _____ by_____ (date)

by doing _____.

Note: There may be instances when you *do* want to set an avoidance goal. For example, if you are struggling with substance issues, it may be helpful to explicitly state what you are attempting to avoid (e.g., goal = no alcohol). Even if complete abstinence is not your goal, you may want to set some rules around your intake of alcohol, such as no alcohol from Mondays to Fridays, and one drink only on weekends and/or special occasions.

Please be mindful that there are 24 hours in a day. Working toward your new goal, whether it is exercising, getting more sleep, or organizing, means that you have less time for something else. If you are adding a one-hour walk every night after dinner, what will you be doing less of (e.g., scrolling through Instagram or Facebook, watching multiple episodes on Netflix)? One place you do not want to compromise is your sleep. My suggestion is to start by reflecting on your cell phone usage; look at the actual number of minutes or hours you are spending on your phone. Maybe you can shave away some time here.

If you have ever had to set goals in a workplace setting, you may be familiar with the concept of SMART (Specific, Measurable, Attainable, Relevant, Time-based) goals, a framework developed by George Doran (1981), as depicted in Table 6. If you have a "bigger" goal (e.g., running a marathon, organizing your home, writing an essay), you will want to break it down into smaller and incremental steps. Running a marathon is not something to take lightly. You can start by looking online to find a schedule that can help you prepare; there are numerous free resources to help you achieve these types of goals. You may also benefit from working with a coach. If you want to organize your home, you may feel overwhelmed and not have the motivation to start. By breaking the task down into mini-tasks (if it is room-by-room), the bigger goal appears more manageable. The same principle can be applied to writing an essay. Break it down into manageable steps/tasks (e.g., research a topic, write a thesis statement, structure your arguments, create an outline of your paper, and so on). Start tackling each step, and you will soon realize that you are moving toward your bigger goal and actually writing your paper.

TABLE 6: SMART GOALS

S: SPECIFIC	Be as specific/narrow as possible. Who? What? Where? When? Why?
M: MEASURABLE	How will you measure your goal? How will you know you are making progress toward your goal? (How much? How often? How many?) It should be very clear to you that you have achieved your goal for that day.
A: ATTAINABLE	Your goal should be challenging but achievable. Circle: Yes or No
R: RELEVANT	Is it relevant to your ultimate goal? Does it align with your values and your long-term goals (e.g., wanting to be healthy)? Does it fit with your identity? Focus on the person you want to become. Circle: Yes or No
T: TIME-BOUND	By when? Date: _____

Try it!

Ultimate goal: _____

Step	Description of Activity	Start Date	Completion Date	Celebration
1				
2				
3				
4				
5				

CREATING HABITS

In best-selling author Charles Duhigg's book *The Power of Habit* (2012), he offers a model that helps individuals build habits. In Duhigg's model, the goal is to turn an activity or exercise into a habit because habits reduce our reliance on mental and physical resources and energy to make them happen. Instead of exerting energy in making multiple mini-decisions—"Should I exercise today? If so, when and for how long? What should I wear? Should I go to my basement and stream a video workout or get outside?"—the decision is already made for you: "It is 7 am on Tuesday; time to put on my sweatpants and tank top and head downstairs for my 30-minute leg workout." Less energy, fewer resources! So how do we get there?

Duhigg's Cue-Routine-Reward model

In this model, he describes the habit loop: Cue → Routine → Reward.

FIGURE 14: THE HABIT LOOP

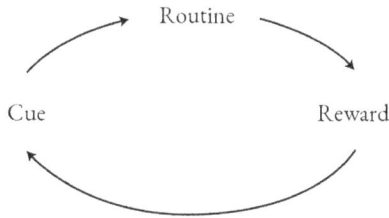

Source: Adapted from Duhigg (2012)

For your interest, a competing model is offered by James Clear in his book *Atomic Habits*. His model has its basis in Duhigg's model and one offered by Nir Eyal in his book *Hooked*.

A. Creating NEW Habits

To understand habit formation, we need to identify the components in Duhigg's (2012) cycle:

1. *The cue:* Every habit starts with a cue or trigger. What is the cue(s) that will start this process? Some cues are *external*, such as the time of day, location, preceding action, or other people, and other cues are *internal*, such as a particular emotional or physiological state (Duhigg, 2012). If you want to start an exercise routine, what will be your cue(s)? Perhaps it will be the time of day—as soon as you wake up you put on your workout clothes and head outside. Remember, as Duhigg explains, we want to limit the resources and energy needed to start the process. Any decision-making/behaviours that can be decided or acted upon in advance will make it easier for you to start forming this habit. At 6 am, there is no decision that needs to be made; *now* is when you have decided to run! What else can you can do in advance to lessen the mental and physical energy needed to run in the morning? Can you lay out your workout clothes the night before? Are your running shoes ready for you at the door? If you are planning to start a gym routine, make sure your bag is packed in advance and that your water bottle is filled. Years ago, when I was regularly running every morning, I sometimes would go to sleep with my exercise clothes on—one less thing to do in the morning! Another example is washing and cutting

your fruits and veggies as soon as you get home from the grocery store. If you open your fridge and you see that the celery and carrots still need to be washed, peeled, and cut, you may be more inclined to grab a bag of chips because it's easier. The planning and prep work is likely to pay off.

2. *The reward:* In Duhigg's cycle, a new behaviour needs a reward. What is the reward for your new behaviour? Is it an intrinsic or *internal* reward, like feeling great completing a run, or is it an extrinsic or *external* reward, such as a treat—a delicious smoothie or a piece of dark chocolate you enjoy after completing a workout? Experiment with these rewards. What will keep you coming back to this activity? Perhaps you will start with an extrinsic reward and then be primarily motivated by intrinsic ones, as working out aligns with something you value, such as a healthy lifestyle. When you first start an exercise routine, you may have days when you do not feel very accomplished at the end of the workout. But as you build your endurance and stamina, and feel your body getting stronger, you may be motivated to engage in your exercise routine to achieve these good feelings and results. Think about other examples as well. If you are a parent, teacher, or caregiver, how can you get your kids, students, or clients to initiate a desirable behaviour? Perhaps you want your child to make their bed and tidy their room every morning. To get started, you may give them a reward such as a sticker when they complete this task. But with time, you phase out the stickers. Research shows that intrinsic rewards, in comparison to extrinsic ones, are powerful motivators of behaviour. But sometimes introducing extrinsic rewards to initiate an activity can help us get started.

3. *The routine:* So now it is time to put Duhigg's advice all together.

    *   What is your cue/trigger? What will set the behaviour in motion? Is it something *internal* (e.g., an emotional or physiological state) or *external* (e.g., time of day, location, other people, or the preceding event)?

    *   What is your reward? Again, is it something *internal* (e.g., a satisfied feeling of accomplishment) or *external* (e.g., a piece of dark chocolate)?

    *   And what will you need to do (the behaviour) to achieve the reward?

The most important part, Duhigg says, is the planning phase. Set a plan for yourself. What will this new habit look like? Write it down and be as specific as possible.

When _____ (cue),

I will _____ (routine)

because it provides me with _____ (reward).

One point to highlight is that it's important to just get started. We have the best intentions regarding what we *want* to do. Our "one days" and "tomorrows" look ideal. I may choose to open another bag of chips or skip a walk or run today, but tomorrow will be different! My intention may be to start running at 6 am *starting tomorrow*. Then, 6 am rolls around and I don't want to get out of bed. What you will learn is that the most difficult part in creating a habit is *getting started*. James Clear (2018) refers to the "two-minute rule"—"when you start a habit, it should take less than two minutes to do." The idea is to make it as easy as possible to *start* the habit. To work toward your bigger goal, start with something that you can definitely do, such as meditating for one minute, or reading one page of your textbook. Perhaps you don't feel like going for a 30-minute run this morning, but can you commit to getting in a 2-minute walk? Clear explains, "Once you've started doing the right thing, it is much easier to continue doing it." Research shows that if you can just get started, you are likely to follow through with the "larger" behaviour. The next time you are just not "feeling it," do it anyway, even for just two minutes. Chances are, you will roll right past that two-minute mark, and you will keep on going.

B. Changing OLD Habits

Duhigg (2012) offers a three-step process to change any current routine:

Step 1. Isolate the cue.

What is/are the cue(s) that will start this process in motion? Recall that cues can vary. Some cues are internal, and others are external. Duhigg recommends that you keep a journal and record these details until you identify the cue(s) for your habit.

- *Location:* Where are you?
- *Time:* What time is it?

- *Emotional state:* How are you feeling? Tired, bored, happy?

- *Other people:* Are you alone or with another person(s)? If the latter, who are you with?

- *Immediately preceding action:* What were you just doing?

After a few days, review your entries. Are there any commonalities? Do you experience this urge at a particular time of day (e.g., mid-afternoon)? Are you hanging around certain people?

Step 2. Experiment with rewards.

What craving do you think this habit is satisfying? Think like a scientist and test your theories! This may take some time, even a few days or weeks. Each day, experiment with a different reward. Consider an example offered in Duhigg's (2012) book: his "cookie problem." Every day at work, mid-afternoon, he would get up from his desk and head to the cafeteria to buy a cookie. Duhigg recommends that to change a current routine, you try something else to attempt to isolate and test each reward. Given the cookie problem, on Day 1, you buy another item, something sweet, in the cafeteria and go back to your desk. On Day 2, you buy a healthy item and then go back to your desk. On Day 3, you skip the trip to the cafeteria, and you head to your friend's desk to chat for 10 minutes. You keep on going until you isolate what is driving the behaviour. Are you taking a break and eating the cookie because you are hungry? If so, perhaps another food item will do the trick. Do you need a break to socialize? If so, chatting with a friend without the cookie would satisfy the craving. Just as you did when trying to isolate the cue, Duhigg suggests journalling after each "experiment." Wait 15 minutes, then reflect on how you are now feeling. Does the reward—the cookie, the apple, talking to a friend—satisfy the craving or not?

Coming back to Duhigg's example, after conducting his experiments, he realized that his craving had nothing to do with hunger, but instead with socializing. As a result, he changed his routine moving forward. Instead of eating a cookie, he took a 10-minute break to chat with a colleague. Craving satisfied!

Step 3. Have a plan.

The key to changing behaviour is to keep the same cue and reward, but to change the routine (Duhigg, 2012).

Here is another example: Imagine that whenever you feel stressed, anxious, or overwhelmed, you reach for an alcoholic drink. The reward for this habit is the relief it brings. Perhaps you have some personal examples that achieve the same result, such as eating snacks, shopping, or scrolling through Instagram. The goal is to find another routine that will achieve the same result or reward. By working through the previous steps (identifying the cue and experimenting with rewards), can you find another behaviour that will suffice? Maybe getting out for a walk with a friend, working out, or meditating will lead to the same reward of stress relief. Start experimenting!

And before we leave this topic, here are a few other tips to consider:

- *Change your identity.* James Clear encourages us to ask this simple question: *What kind of person do I want to become?* By aligning your goal to a value (e.g., health), you are more likely to stick to your goals. For example, "I want to run/walk and/or lift weights so that I can become a healthier me." Other examples that he offers include wanting to become the type of person "who moves more every day," "who writes 1,000 words every day," "who always stays in touch," or "who is always on time." For more information on identity-based habits, see Clear's book *Atomic Habits.*

- *Believe that change is possible.* Adopting a growth mindset when it comes to creating new or replacing old habits is crucial. If you believe that change is not possible, that the effort is not worth it (fixed mindset), you are setting yourself up for failure even before you start. Starting small and making tiny, incremental gains will lead to change, as those 1% shifts toward your bigger goal will add up (Clear, 2018).

- *Anticipate challenges.* You will benefit from doing the thinking work beforehand. We can make decisions for ourselves that help us stick to our goals. For example, take another route to work to avoid the doughnut shop along the way. Or avoid the aisles at the grocery store with items that tempt you. But sometimes we find ourselves in situations where temptation is in front of us. In these cases, you can set *implementation intentions* (if-then statements) as suggested by Clear (2018). Anticipate the challenges along the way! For example, before you find yourself in tempting situations, you can set an implementation intention by stating, "*If* I am offered a dessert menu, *then* I will ask for an herbal tea instead." Or "*If* I am offered an alcoholic drink at a party, *then* I will request a non-alcoholic spritzer instead." By making the decision beforehand, you do not need to use your limited resources and contemplate the decision (Do I have just one drink? If so, which one?), because the decision has already been made.

Try it!

If _____,

then _____.

If _____,

then _____.

If _____,

then _____.

- *Tie your new behaviour to an existing habit.* This is another application of an implementation intention, because you are creating a cue/trigger for your new behaviour (Clear, 2018). For example, if you get up in the morning and make coffee, take this opportunity to engage in a five-minute meditation (make coffee → five-minute meditation). Or when brushing or flossing your teeth at night, you can tack on a gratitude practice (brush/floss teeth at night → recall three things that I am grateful for that happened during the day).

- *Try to stick to your schedule, even in small ways.* Even if you do not have the time or energy to engage in the behaviour that is on your schedule, make the choice to do a small part of it (Clear, n.d.). If your intention is to walk at least one hour every day, but you don't have a full hour today because of meetings or appointments, can you squeeze in 10 minutes? Instead of scrapping the entire routine, it is more important to be consistent with your intention, even if only for a few minutes. If there is a way to plan ahead, do it! Remember, half the battle is in the planning. Spend the time doing the work beforehand and reap the benefits. And if you don't "feel like it" because you are too tired or overwhelmed, do a small part of it anyway!

- *Limit distraction/temptation as much as possible.* Do you find the "pings" and constant notifications coming through your phone are taking you away from the task at hand? Turn them off! Do you want to cut down on mindless scrolling on your phone? Remove your phone from view!

Do you have a cookie jar out on a countertop? Get it out of there—or better yet, don't buy the cookies! *Out of sight, out of mind.* Think about the environment you are creating around you—is it conducive to your success?

- *Create rules for yourself.* Do you find yourself checking email multiple times throughout the day? You may consider only checking your email three times a day. Are you trying to create a more restful bedtime routine? Make a plan to turn off all devices at a particular time each night (e.g., 10 pm). Do you want to eliminate the amount of snacking you engage in late at night? Set a rule for yourself to not snack after 8 pm, or another time, each night. Think about creating simple rules for yourself that will help you stick to your goals.

- And finally, *remember to celebrate small wins.* How will you reward yourself? To get started, you may want to treat yourself every time you complete the routine. Although intrinsic motivations are key to continued success, these small rewards can give you a bit of pep to get started and keep going. Celebrate the new you that you are becoming!

On a final note, be kind to yourself. Practice self-compassion along the way. Although I have offered you some tips in this section, you will likely find that you struggle from time to time. Most of us do—remember the common humanity aspect of self-compassion. Those of us who are self-compassionate are more likely to move toward and achieve our goals. Take time to acknowledge that you are human and reflect on the factors that got in the way. Plan to do better today, and tomorrow. Again, what appears to be a "person" problem is often a "process" problem. Change your mindset and create or re-create a plan (the process).

CONCLUSION

I don't want to get to the end of my life and find that I have just lived
the length of it. I want to have lived the width of it as well.

~ Diane Ackerman

Your life is made of two dates and a dash.
Make the most of the dash.

~ Linda Ellis

When I started writing this book, my aim was to create a resource that would challenge the way you moved through the world. Throughout this book, I have asked various questions, and I have invited you to engage in some reflective exercises so that you could learn more about you. By reflecting on what matters to you—your values, your strengths, your goals, your mindset, and how you apply your energy and effort in various pursuits—I hope you are walking away from this book with a clearer vision of how you want to live your life and a fuller toolbox to help you navigate the road ahead.

Ellis extends upon her metaphor of the dash from the opening quote in the poem below. Reflect on her words:

I read of a man who stood to speak
at the funeral of a friend
He referred to the dates on the tombstone
from the beginning ... to the end.

He noted that first came the date of birth
and spoke the following date with tears,
but he said what mattered most of all
was the dash between those years.

For that dash represents all the time
that they spent alive on earth.
And now only those who loved them
know what that little line is worth.

For it matters not, how much we own—
the cars ... the house ... the cash.
What matters is how we live and love
and how we spend our dash.

So, think about this long and hard.
Are there things you'd like to change?
For you never know how much time is left
that can still be rearranged.

If we could just slow down enough
to consider what's true and real,
and always try to understand
the way other people feel.

And be less quick to anger
and show appreciation more,
and love the people in our lives
like we've never loved before.

If we treat each other with respect
and more often wear a smile,
remembering this special dash
might only last a little while.

So, when your eulogy is being read
with your life's actions to rehash,
would you be proud of the things they say
about how you spent your dash?

(Ellis, 2011)

What is truly important in your life right now, and in the future? Is what is happening in this moment, if uncomfortable, *really* going to matter at the very end of your time on earth? Sometimes it's difficult to navigate a challenging situation or emotion; self-defeating narratives take over and suck the air out of the present moment. Can you pause … take a breath … and create space as you approach what is in front of and within you with a curious mind and open heart? Can you ride the wave of an edgy emotion? Can you remind yourself that most things will not feel the same way down the line, as you acknowledge the impermanence of a situation and an emotion? Over the years, I have come to realize the greyness and ambiguity in most circumstances as there are multiple ways to see and interpret most situations. I am committed to bringing this curious mind and gracious heart as I navigate this ambiguity as I experiment with different lenses and I try to better understand my inner and outer world. I hope you are inspired to do the same as well. I believe that this softer and more mindful approach is desperately needed in the world today. Let us commit to doing our best, knowing that we will mess up and make mistakes along the way. The important thing is that we approach these situations with kindness and compassion (for ourselves and others), make amends (if applicable), and strive to learn and do better next time.

In Bronnie Ware's book *The Top 5 Regrets of the Dying* (2019), she did just that as she listened to the stories of her dying patients. With this temporal lens in mind, what truly matters in the end? Here is what she found:

1. I wish I'd had the courage to live a life true to myself, not the life others expected of me.

2. I wish I hadn't worked so hard.

3. I wish I'd had the courage to express my feelings.

4. I wish I had stayed in touch with my friends.

5. I wish I had let myself be happier.

Take note of #5 on this list: *I wish I had let myself be happier.* Grant yourself permission to engage in replenishing activities that support your well-being and happiness and allow you to do the amazing work that you do—with energy, passion, and conviction! Remember, "Taking good care of you means the people in your life will receive the best of you, rather than what's left of you."

What makes *your* list? What are the things in your life that matter to you? Many of these activities that are important and meaningful to us, such as caregiving responsibilities, committee work, and social justice activities, can drain our energy reserves if we do not take care of ourselves. Be choosy when deciding how you spend your energy!

MY LIST OF THINGS THAT TRULY MATTER
List things that are worth the cost of your time and energy.

And what *doesn't* make this list?

MY LIST OF THINGS THAT ARE NOT WORTH THE COST OF MY TIME AND ENERGY

List things here—both thoughts and actions—that you are currently pouring your time and energy into and that upon reflection are not worth their high energy price tag.

Once you have set your priorities, how can you ensure that you have the energy to put into these activities? Many of the activities from List 1 that are important or meaningful to you draw on your energy reserves. Reflect on some of the WOW tips. How do you fill your energy tank? Check those that resonate with you and prioritize them by ranking them. Remember, if you are adding something to your list—like an extra hour of sleep, 30 minutes of exercise, or 10 minutes of meditation—something must come off your list. It is a zero-sum game—there are only 24 hours in the day!

ENERGY-ENHANCING ACTIVITIES

☐ Sleep: _____ hours per day

☐ Exercise: _____ minutes per day

☐ Gratitude journal

☐ Meditate: _____ minutes per day

☐ Spending time with family or friends

☐ Practice self-care (specify): _____

☐ Other: _____

☐ Other: _____

☐ Other: _____

☐ Other: _____

☐ Other: _____

☐ Other: _____

☐ Other: _____

ENERGY-DEPLETING LIST

What will you do less of or eliminate altogether to make space in your calendar for these energy-enhancing activities?

☐ Less time on social media

☐ Checking email less often

☐ Less time spent watching TV/Netflix...

☐ Other: _____

☐ Other: _____

☐ Other: _____

☐ Other: _____

☐ Other: _____

☐ Other: _____

☐ Other: _____

And now it is your turn. As you journey forward, I hope you have a fuller toolbox as you move toward the goals that matter most to you, and that you encounter each moment along your path with a curious mind and open heart. Embrace the pause and find solace and grounding in your breath and/or body as you continue to learn, stretch, and *bend*. Be flexible as you decide how to spend this invaluable resource, as you keep coming back to this basic question in each moment: *Is this how I want to spend my energy?* That is the essence of bendABILITY, the moment-by-moment choice of if and when to bend and exert energy and effort as you create a meaningFULL life worth living.

ABOUT THE AUTHOR

Carla LaBella is a professor of psychology in the School of Liberal Studies at Mohawk College. She teaches a variety of psychology-related courses (including Introductory Psychology, Positive Psychology, Abnormal Psychology, and Human Sexuality) to various programs within the College and, until recently, to the Collaborative Nursing (BScN) program at McMaster University. She is the co-facilitator and co-founder of the Happiness (Wellness) Series for students and staff, and she offers a number of wellness sessions throughout the college and in the greater Hamilton community. Outside the college, she is a board member for the Suicide Prevention Community Council of Hamilton (SPCCH), the Hamilton Program for Schizophrenia (HPS), and Mindfulness Hamilton. She earned her honours BA in psychology from McMaster University (1997) and MA in cognitive psychology from the University of Waterloo (2000). She also obtained a certificate in applied positive psychology (CAPP) from the Flourishing Center (2014), and became a Unified Mindfulness coach (Pathways for Teaching Mindfulness, Foundations of UM) in 2021 and a Modo Yoga teacher (Level 1—200-hour teacher training) in 2022. Recently, she was the recipient of the Award for Excellence in Full-Time Teaching—Local 240 (2022) and the Jacqui Candlish Award for Excellence in Suicide Prevention Work (2019), and she was a nominee for the YWCA Women of Distinction award (2018). Aside from being a teacher, she is a yoga enthusiast, avid nonfiction reader, a mom to two active boys, and a partner to her husband.

REFERENCES

Al-Saggaf, Y., & O'Donnell, S. (2019). Phubbing: Perceptions, reasons behind, predictors, and impacts. *Human Behavior and Emerging Technologies, 1*(2), 132–140. https://doi.org/10.1002/hbe2.137

Amortegui, J. (2015, November 17). The secret to more meaningful work. *Forbes*. https://www.forbes.com/sites/womensmedia/2015/11/17/the-secret-to-more-meaningful-work/?sh=cc777015116a

Andrews, P., & Thomson, J. (2009). The bright side of being blue: Depression as an adaptation for analyzing complex problems. *Psychological Review, 116*(3), 620–654. https://doi.org/10.1037/a0016242

Angus Reid Institute. (2019, June 17). *A portrait of social isolation and loneliness in Canada today*. https://angusreid.org/social-isolation-loneliness-canada/

Baiyekusi, I., & Prasad, D. (2016). Neuroplasticity in play: Outcomes after hemispherectomy in Rasmussen encephalitis. *Indian Journal of Neurosciences, 2*(3), 56–59. https://www.academia.edu/29611205/Neuroplasticity_in_play_Outcomes_after_Hemispherectomy_in_Rasmussen_Encephalitis

Bargh, J., & Melnikoff, D. (2019). Commentary: Does physical warmth prime social warmth? Reply to Chabris et al. (2019). *Social Psychology, 50*(3), 207–210. https://doi.org/10.1027/1864-9335/a000387

Ben-Shahar, T. (2007). *Happier: Learn the secrets to daily joy and lasting fulfillment*. McGraw-Hill.

Berg, J. M., Dutton, J. E., & Wrzesniewski, A. (2008). *What is job crafting and why does it matter?* Regents of the University of Michigan. http://positiveorgs.bus.umich.edu/wp-content/uploads/What-is-Job-Crafting-and-Why-Does-it-Matter1.pdf

Bolte Taylor, J. (2009). *My stroke of insight: A brain scientist's personal journey*. Penguin.

Bonanno, G. (2004). Loss, trauma, and human resilience: Have we underestimated the human capacity to thrive after extremely adverse events? *American Psychologist, 59*(1), 20–28. https://doi.org/10.1037/0003-066x.59.1.20

Bonanno, G. (2021). The resilience paradox. *European Journal of Psychotraumatology*, *12*(1), 1–8. https://doi.org/10.1080/20008198.2021.1942642

Boniwell, I. (2012). *Positive psychology in a nutshell: The science of happiness* (3rd ed.). Open University Press.

Brach, T. (2020a). *Radical compassion: Learning to love yourself and your world with the practice of RAIN*. Penguin Life.

Brach, T. (2020b). RAIN: A practice of radical compassion. *Tara Brach*. https://www.tarabrach.com/rain-practice-radical-compassion/

Brickman, P., & Campbell, D. (1971). Hedonic relativism and planning the good society. In M. Appley (Ed.), *Adaptation-level theory: A symposium* (pp. 287–305). Academic Press.

Brickman, P., Coates, D., & Janoff-Bulman, R. (1978). Lottery winners and accident victims: Is happiness relative? *Journal of Personality and Social Psychology*, *36*(8), 917–927. https://doi.org/10.1037/0022-3514.36.8.917

Brown, B. (2010). *Gifts of imperfection: Let go of who you think you're supposed to be and embrace who you are*. Hazelden.

Brown, B. (2012a). *Daring greatly: How the courage to be vulnerable transforms the way we live, love, parent, and lead*. Gotham Books.

Brown, B. (2012b). *Listening to shame* [Video]. TED. https://www.ted.com/talks/brene_brown_listening_to_shame

Brown, B. (2013, December 10). *Brené Brown on empathy* [Video]. YouTube. https://www.youtube.com/watch?v=1Evwgu369Jw

Brown, N., & Rohrer, J. (2020). Easy as (happiness) pie? A critical evaluation of a popular model of the determinants of well-being. *Journal of Happiness Studies: An Interdisciplinary Forum on Subjective Well-Being, 21*(4), 1285–1301. https://link.springer.com/article/10.1007/s10902-019-00128-4

Brown, N., & Rohrer, J. (2021). Correction to: Easy as (happiness) pie? A critical evaluation of a popular model of the determinants of well-being. *Journal of Happiness Studies*, *23*(3), 1307–1307. https://doi.org/10.1007/s10902-021-00408-y

Brown, N., Sokal, A., & Friedman, H. (2013). The complex dynamics of wishful thinking: The critical positivity ratio. *The American Psychologist, 68*(9), 801–813. https://doi.org/10.1037/a0032850

Cacioppo, J. (2013, September 9). *The lethality of loneliness: John Cacioppo at TEDxDesMoines* [Video]. YouTube. https://www.youtube.com/watch?v=_0hx-l03JoA0

Cameron, K. (2008). Paradox in positive organizational change. *The Journal of Applied Behavioral Science, 44*(1), 7–24. https://doi.org/10.1177/0021886308314703

Canadian Society for Exercise Physiology. (2021). *24-hour movement guidelines.* https://csepguidelines.ca/downloads/

Carney, D., Cuddy, A., & Yap, A. (2010). Power posing: Brief nonverbal displays affect neuroendocrine levels and risk tolerance. *Psychological Science, 21*(10):1363–8. https://pubmed.ncbi.nlm.nih.gov/20855902/

Centers for Disease Control and Prevention. (2020, October 14). *Target heart rate and estimated maximum heart rate.* https://www.cdc.gov/physicalactivity/basics/measuring/heartrate.htm

Chabris, C., Heck, P., Mandart, J., Benjamin, D., & Simons, D. (2019). No evidence that experiencing physical warmth promotes interpersonal warmth: Two failures to replicate. *Social Psychology, 50*(2), 127–132. https://doi.org/10.1027/1864-9335/a000361

Chaput, J., Dutil, C., & Sampasa-Kanyinga, H. (2018). Sleeping hours: What is the ideal number and how does age impact this? *Nature and Science of Sleep, 10,* 421–430. https://doi.org/10.2147/NSS.S163071

Clear, J. (2018). *Atomic habits: An easy & proven way to build good habits & break bad ones.* Avery.

Clear, J. (n.d.). *3 time management tips that actually work.* JAMES CLEAR. https://jamesclear.com/time-management-tips

Cleveland Clinic. (2022, September 7). *How and why to try alternate nostril breathing.* HealthEssentials. https://health.clevelandclinic.org/alternate-nostril-breathing/

Coles, N., Larsen, J., & Lench, H. (2019). A meta-analysis of the facial feedback literature: Effects of facial feedback on emotional experience are small and variable. *Psychological Bulletin*, *145*(6), 610–651. https://doi.org/10.1037/bul0000194

Cuddy, A. (2015). *Presence: Bringing your boldest self to your biggest challenges.* Little, Brown & Company.

Cuddy, A., Wilmuth, C., Yap, A., & Carney, D. (2015). Preparatory power posing affects nonverbal presence and job interview performance. *Journal of Applied Psychology, 100*(4), 1286–1295. https://pubmed.ncbi.nlm.nih.gov/25664473/

Cuddy, A., Schultz, S., & Fosse, N. (2018). P-curving a more comprehensive body of research on postural feedback reveals clear evidential value for power-posing effects: Reply to Simmons and Simonsohn (2017). *Psychological Science*, *29*(4), 656–666. https://journals.sagepub.com/eprint/CzbNAn7Ch6ZZirK9yMGH/full

Danner, D., Snowdon, D., & Friesen, W. (2001). Positive emotions in early life and longevity: Findings from the nun study. *Journal of Personality and Social Psychology*, *80*(5), 804–813. https://doi.org/10.1037//0022-3514.80.5.804

Davis, D., & Hayes, J. (2012). What are the benefits of mindfulness? *Monitor on Psychology*, *43*(7). https://www.apa.org/monitor/2012/07-08/ce-corner

Deaton, A., & Stone, A. (2014). Evaluative and hedonic wellbeing among those with and without children at home. *Proceedings of the National Academy of Sciences of the United States of America*, *111*(4), 1328–1333. https://doi.org/10.1073/pnas.1311600111

Delehanty, H. (2017, December 13). The science of meditation. *Mindful.* https://www.mindful.org/meditators-under-the-microscope/

Devi, G. (2012). *A calm brain: How to relax into a stress-free, high-powered life.* Penguin.

Dimberg, U., Thunberg, M., & Elmehed, K. (2000). Unconscious facial reactions to emotional facial expressions. *Psychological Science*, *11*(1), 86–89. https://doi.org/10.1111/1467-9280.00221

Doidge, N. (2007). *The brain that changes itself: Stories of personal triumph from the frontiers of brain science.* Penguin.

Doidge, N. (2015). *The brain's way of healing: Remarkable discoveries and recoveries from the frontiers of neuroplasticity.* Viking.

Doran, G. (1981). There's a S.M.A.R.T. way to write management's goals and objectives. *Management Review, 70*(11), 35–36. https://community.mis. temple.edu/mis0855002fall2015/files/2015/10/S.M.A.R.T-Way-Management-Review.pdf

Drouin, M., Kaiser, D., & Miller, D. (2012, July). Phantom vibrations in young adults: Prevalence and underlying psychological characteristics. *Computers in Human Behaviour, 28*(4), 1490–1496. https://www.sciencedirect.com/science/article/abs/pii/S0747563212000799

Duckworth, S. (2019). *Sketchnotes for educators: 100 inspiring illustrations for lifelong learners.* Elevate Books.

Duhigg, C. (2012). *The power of habit: Why we do what we do in life and business.* Random House.

Dunn, E, Aknin, L., & Norton, M. (2008). Spending money on others promotes happiness. *Science, 319*, 1687–1688. https://doi.org/10.1126/science.1150952

Dweck, C. (2007). *Mindset: The new psychology of success.* Ballantine.

Ellis, L. (2011). *Live your dash: Make every moment matter.* Sterling Ethos.

Emmons, R. (2010, November 16). Why gratitude is good. *Greater Good Magazine.* http://greatergood.berkeley.edu/article/item/why_gratitude_is_good/

Emmons, R., & McCullough, M. (2003). Counting blessings versus burdens: An experimental investigation of gratitude and subjective well-being in daily life. *Journal of Personality and Social Psychology, 84*(2), 377–389. https://doi.org/10.1037//0022-3514.84.2.377

Emmons, R., & Shelton, C. (2002). Gratitude and the science of positive psychology. In C. Snyder and S. Lopez (Eds.), *Handbook of positive psychology* (pp. 459–471). Oxford University Press.

Enten, H. (2022, May 28). It turns out money may buy some happiness. *CNN.* https://www.cnn.com/2022/05/28/health/money-happiness-wellness/index.html

Farmer Sean. (2018, July 1). Two monks and a woman — zen story. *Medium.* https://medium.com/@soninilucas/two-monks-and-a-woman-zen-story-c15294c394c1

Fogel, A. (2012, April 19). Emotional and physical pain activate similar brain regions. *Psychology Today.* https://www.psychologytoday.com/ca/blog/body-sense/201204/emotional-and-physical-pain-activate-similar-brain-regions

Foster, D. (2016, January 23). Is mindfulness making us ill? *The Guardian.* https://www.theguardian.com/lifeandstyle/2016/jan/23/is-mindfulness-making-us-ill

Fredrickson, B. (2009). *Positivity: Discover the upward spiral that will change your life.* Three Rivers Press.

Fredrickson, B. (2011, June 21). Are you getting enough positivity in your diet? *Greater Good Magazine.* https://greatergood.berkeley.edu/article/item/are_you_getting_enough_positivity_in_your_diet

Fredrickson, B. (2004). The broaden-and-build theory of positive emotions. *Philosophical Transactions of the Royal Society of London. Series B, Biological Sciences, 359,* 1367–1378. https://doi.org/10.1098/rstb.2004.1512

Fredrickson, B. (2013). Updated thinking on positivity ratios. *The American Psychologist, 68*(9), 814–822. https://doi.org/10.1037/a0033584

Fredrickson, B., Cohn, M., Coffey, K., Pek, J., & Finkel, S. (2008). Open hearts build lives: Positive emotions, induced through loving-kindness meditation, build consequential personal resources. *Journal of Personality and Social Psychology, 95*(5), 1045–1062. https://doi.org/10.1037/a0013262

Gable, S., Gonzaga, G., & Strachman, A. (2006). Will you be there for me when things go right? Supportive responses to positive event disclosures. *Journal of Personality and Social Psychology, 91*(5), 904–917. https://doi.org/10.1037/0022-3514.91.5.904

Gallup. (2006, June 8). Too many interruptions at work. *Business Journal.* https://news.gallup.com/businessjournal/23146/too-many-interruptions-work.aspx

Germer, C. (2009). *The mindful path to self-compassion: Freeing yourself from destructive thoughts and emotions.* Guilford Press.

Gerritsen, R., & Band, G. (2018). Breath of life: The respiratory vagal stimulation model of contemplative activity. *Frontiers in Human Neuroscience, 12,* 1–25. https://doi.org/10.3389/fnhum.2018.00397

Gilovich, T., Kumar, A., & Jampol, L. (2015). A wonderful life: Experiential consumption and the pursuit of happiness. *Journal of Consumer Psychology: The Official Journal of the Society for Consumer Psychology, 25*(1), 152–165. https://doi.org/10.1016/j.jcps.2014.08.004

Glikson, E., Cheshin, A., & Van Kleef, G. (2018). The dark side of a smiley: Effects of smiling emoticons on virtual first impressions. *Social Psychological and Personality Science, 9*(5), 614–625. https://doi.org/10.1177/1948550617720269

Goleman, D., & Davidson, R. (2018). *Altered traits: Science reveals how meditation changes your mind, brain, and body.* Avery.

Gottman, J., & Silver, N. (2000). *The seven principles for making marriage work: A practical guide from the country's foremost relationship expert.* Harmony.

Greater Good In Action. (n.d.). *Self-compassionate letter.* https://ggia.berkeley.edu/practice/self_compassionate_letter

Halifax, J. (2009). *Being with dying: Cultivating compassion and fearlessness in the presence of death.* Shambhala.

Halifax, J. (2018). *Standing at the edge: Finding freedom where fear and courage meet.* Flatiron Books.

Hall, K. (2012, April 26). Understanding validation: A way to communicate acceptance. *Psychology Today.* https://www.psychologytoday.com/ca/blog/pieces-mind/201204/understanding-validation-way-communicate-acceptance

Hạnh, T. (1999). *The heart of the Buddha's teaching: Transforming suffering into peace, joy, and liberation.* Harmony.

Hari, J. (2019). *Lost connections: Why you're depressed and how to find hope.* Bloomsbury.

Harris, R. (2008). *Values worksheet (adapted from Kelly Wilson's valued living questionnaire).* The happiness trap. http://thehappinesstrap.com/upimages/Values_Questionnaire.pdf

Harris, R. (2010). *A quick look at your values - page 1.* ACT Mindfully Workshops with Russ Harris. http://www.actmindfully.com.au/wp-content/uploads/2019/07/Values_Checklist_-_Russ_Harris.pdf

Hatfield, E., Cacioppo, J., & Rapson, R. (1993). Emotional contagion. *Current Directions in Psychological Science, 2,* 96–99. https://www.jstor.org/stable/20182211

Hicks, J., & Martela, F. (2022, April 15). A new dimension to a meaningful life. *Scientific American.* https://www.scientificamerican.com/article/a-new-dimension-to-a-meaningful-life1/

Hofmann, S., Asnaani, A., Vonk, I., Sawyer, A., & Fang, A. (2019). The efficacy of cognitive behavioral therapy: A review of meta-analyses. *Cognitive Therapy and Research, 36*(5), 427–440. https://www.academia.edu/24714435/The_Efficacy_of_Cognitive_Behavioral_Therapy-_A_Review_of_Meta_analyses

Hogue, J., & Mills, J. (2019). The effects of active social media engagement with peers on body image in young women. *Body Image, 28,* 1–5. https://doi.org/10.1016/j.bodyim.2018.11.002

Hunt, M., Marx, R., Lipson, C., & Young, J. (2018). No more FOMO: Limiting social media decreases loneliness and depression. *Journal of Social and Clinical Psychology, 37*(10), 751–768. https://doi.org/10.1521/jscp.2018.37.10.751

Hutson, M. (2015, January 6). Beyond happiness: The upside of feeling down. *Psychology Today.* https://www.psychologytoday.com/us/articles/201501/beyond-happiness-the-upside-feeling-down

Indigenous Fellowship of Hamilton Road. (n.d.). *Medicine wheel.* https://ifhr.ca/medicine-wheel/

Joseph, S. (2014, December 7). Humanistic and positive psychology. *Psychology Today.* https://www.psychologytoday.com/ca/blog/what-doesnt-kill-us/201412/humanistic-and-positive-psychology

Kahneman, D. (2013). *Thinking fast and slow*. Anchor Canada.

Kahneman, D., & Deaton, A. (2010). High income improves evaluation of life but not emotional well-being. *Proceedings of the National Academy of Sciences of the United States of America, 107*(38), 16489–16493. https://doi.org/10.1073/pnas.1011492107

Karlsson, H. (2011, August 12). How psychotherapy changes the brain. *Psychiatric Times, 28*(8). https://www.psychiatrictimes.com/view/how-psychotherapy-changes-brain

Kashdan, T., & Mcknight, P. (2009). Origins of purpose in life: Refining our understanding of a life well lived. *Psychological Topics, 18*, 303–316. https://hrcak.srce.hr/file/74339

Kashdan, T., & Breen, W. (2007). Materialism and diminished well–being: Experiential avoidance as a mediating mechanism. *Journal of Social and Clinical Psychology, 26*(5), 521–539. https://doi.org/10.1521/jscp.2007.26.5.521

Killingsworth, M. (2021). Experienced well-being rises with income, even above $75,000 per year. *Proceedings of the National Academy of Sciences of the United States of America, 118*(4), 1–6. https://doi.org/10.1073/pnas.2016976118

Killingsworth, M., & Gilbert, D. (2010). A wandering mind is an unhappy mind. *Science, 330*, 932–932. https://doi.org/10.1126/science.1192439

Lawton, R., Gramatki, I., Watt, W., & Fujiwara, D. (2020). Does volunteering make us happier, or are happier people more likely to volunteer? Addressing the problem of reverse causality when estimating the wellbeing impacts of volunteering. *Journal of Happiness Studies, 22*(2), 599–624. https://doi.org/10.1007/s10902-020-00242-8

Lewis, M. (2009, February 13). The no-stats all-star. *New York Times*. http://www.nytimes.com/2009/02/15/magazine/15Battier-t.html

Lieberman, M., Eisenberger, N., Crockett, M., Tom, S., Pfeifer, J., & Way, B. (2007). Putting feelings into words: Affect labeling disrupts amygdala activity in response to affective stimuli. *Psychological Science,18*(5), 421–428. https://www.scn.ucla.edu/pdf/AL(2007).pdf

Lin, I., Tai, L., & Fan, S. (2014). Breathing at a rate of 5.5 breaths per minute with equal inhalation-to-exhalation ratio increases heart rate variability. *International Journal of Psychophysiology: Official Journal of the International Organization of Psychophysiology, 91*(3), 206–211. https://doi.org/10.1016/j.ijpsycho.2013.12.006

Loehr, J., & Schwartz, T. (2005). *The power of full engagement: Managing energy, not time, is the key to high performance and personal renewal.* Free Press.

Lyubomirsky, S., Sheldon, K., & Schkade, D. (2005). Pursuing happiness: The architecture of sustainable change. *Review of General Psychology: Journal of Division 1, of the American Psychological Association, 9*(2), 111–131. https://doi.org/10.1037/1089-2680.9.2.111

Maguire, E., Gadian, D., Johnsrude, I., Good, C., Ashburner, J., Frackowiak, R., & Frith, C. (2000). Navigation-related structural change in the hippocampi of taxi drivers. *Proceedings of the National Academy of Sciences of the United States of America, 97*(8), 4398–4403. https://www.ncbi.nlm.nih.gov/pmc/articles/PMC18253/

Marchant, J. (2016). Placebos: Honest fakery. *Nature, 535,* S14–S15. https://www.nature.com/articles/535S14a#citeas

Marsh, J. (2012, March 14). The power of self-compassion. *Greater Good Magazine.* http://greatergood.berkeley.edu/article/item/the_power_of_self_compassion

Martela, F., & Steger, M. (2016). The three meanings of meaning in life: Distinguishing coherence, purpose, and significance. *The Journal of Positive Psychology, 11*(5), 531–545. https://doi.org/10.1080/17439760.2015.1137623

Martin, D. (2012). *This is a book.* Grand Central Publishing.

McCall, S. (2018, March 10). Maybe, said the farmer. *Medium.* https://medium.com/@steven.mccall/maybe-said-the-farmer-c6b13bcb5124

McGonigal, K. (2012, June 4). Does self-compassion or criticism motivate self-improvement? *Psychology Today.* https://www.psychologytoday.com/blog/the-science-willpower/201206/does-self-compassion-or-criticism-motivate-self-improvement

McGonigal, K. (2013, June). *How to make stress your friend* [Video]. TED. https://www.ted.com/talks/kelly_mcgonigal_how_to_make_stress_ your_friend

McKnight, P., & Kashdan, T. (2009). Purpose in life as a system that creates and sustains health and well-being: An integrative, testable theory. *Review of General Psychology, 13*, 242–251. https://www.academia. edu/2833030/Purpose_in_life_as_a_system_that_creates_and_sustains_health_and_well_being_An_integrative_testable_theory

McPherson, M., Smith-Lovin, L., & Brashears, M. (2006). Social isolation in America: Changes in core discussion networks over two decades. *American Sociological Review, 71*(3), 353–375. https://doi.org/ 10.1177/000312240607100301

Mills, J., Musto, S., Williams, L., & Tiggemann, M. (2018). "Selfie" harm: Effects on mood and body image in young women. *Body Image, 27*, 86–92. https://doi.org/10.1016/j.bodyim.2018.08.007

Mnyaka, M., & Motlhabi, M. (2005). The African concept of ubuntu/botho and its socio-moral significance. *An International Journal, 3*(2), 215–237. https://doi.org/10.1558/blth.3.2.215.65725

Murthy, V. (2020). *Together: The healing power of human connection in a sometimes lonely world*. HarperCollins.

Neff, K. (n.d.-a). *Definition of self-compassion*. Self-Compassion — Dr. Kristen Neff. http://self-compassion.org/the-three-elements-of-self-compassion-2/

Neff, K. (n.d.-b). *Exercise 1: How would you treat a friend?* Self-Compassion — Dr. Kristen Neff. https://self-compassion.org/exercise-1-treat-friend/

Neff, K. (n.d.-c). *Exercise 2: Self-compassion break*. Self-Compassion — Dr. Kristen Neff. https://self-compassion.org/exercise-2-self-compassion-break/

Neff, K. (n.d.-d). *Exercise 6: Self-compassion journal*. Self-Compassion — Dr. Kristen Neff. https://self-compassion.org/exercise-6-self-compassion-journal/

Neff, K. (n.d.-e). *The physiology of self-compassion*. Self-Compassion — Dr. Kristen Neff. https://self-compassion.org/the-physiology-of-self-compassion/

Nestor, J. (2020). *Breath: The new science of a lost art.* Riverhead.

Nestor, J. (n.d.). *Bibliography & extended notes.* MRJAMESNESTOR. https://www.mrjamesnestor.com/bibliography

Newman, K. (2014, December 22). Variety is the spice of emotional life. *Greater Good Magazine.* http://greatergood.berkeley.edu/article/item/variety_is_the_spice_of_emotional_life

Niemiec, R. (2019). Finding the golden mean: The overuse, underuse, and optimal use of character strengths. *Counselling Psychology Quarterly, 32*(3–4), 453–471. https://doi.org/10.1080/09515070.2019.1617674

Novella, S. (2017, November 15). *Placebo myths debunked.* Science-Based Medicine. https://sciencebasedmedicine.org/placebo-myths-debunked/

PBS. (2016, October 6). *BJ Miller: In facing death, this doctor sees a way to live well* [Video]. PBS News Hour. https://www.pbs.org/newshour/show/facing-death-doctor-sees-way-live-well

Pennebaker, J., & Chung, C. (2012). Expressive writing, emotional upheavals, and health. In H. Friedman (Ed.), *The Oxford handbook of health psychology* (pp. 417–437). Oxford University Press

Pennebaker, J. (1997). Writing about emotional experiences as a therapeutic process. *Psychological Science, 8*(3), 162–166. https://doi.org/10.1111/j.1467-9280.1997.tb00403.x

Peterson, C., & Seligman, M. (2004). *Character strengths and virtues: A handbook and classification.* Oxford.

Quoidbach, J., Gruber, J., Mikolajczak, M., Kogan, A., Kotsou, I., & Norton, M. (2014). Emodiversity and the emotional ecosystem. *Journal of Experimental Psychology: General, 143*(6), 2057–2066. https://doi.org/10.1037/a0038025

Ratey, J., & Hagerman, E. (2008). *Spark: The revolutionary new science of exercise and the brain.* Little, Brown & Company.

Rodriguez, T. (2012, September 1). Botox fights depression. *Scientific American.* https://www.scientificamerican.com/article/botox-fights-depression/

Sarwari, K. (2019, July 19). Northeastern university professor says we can't gauge emotions from facial expressions alone. *Northeastern Global News*. https://news.northeastern.edu/2019/07/19/northeastern-university-professor-says-we-cant-gauge-emotions-from-facial-expressions-alone/

Schaffner, A. (2016, September 5). *How to escape the hedonic treadmill and be happier*. Positivepsychology.com. https://positivepsychology.com/hedonic-treadmill/#google_vignette

Schkade, D., & Kahneman, D. (1998). Does living in California make people happy? A focusing illusion in judgments of life satisfaction. *Psychological Science*, *9*(5), 340–346. https://doi.org/10.1111/1467-9280.00066

Schmidt, M. (2019, September 20). Short sleeper 'syndrome': When you can get by on just a few hours of sleep. *Discover*. https://www.discovermagazine.com/health/short-sleeper-syndrome-when-you-can-get-by-on-just-a-few-hours-of-sleep

Schulte, B. (2015). *Overwhelmed: Work, love, and play when no one has the time*. Picador.

Schwartz, T., & McCarthy, C. (2007). Manage your energy, not your time. *Harvard Business Review*. https://hbr.org/2007/10/manage-your-energy-not-your-time

Seligman, M. (2006). *Learned optimism: How to change your mind and your life*. Vintage.

Seligman, M. (2012). *Flourish: A visionary new understanding of happiness and well-being*. Atria.

Seligman, M. (2015). Chris Peterson's unfinished masterwork: The real mental illnesses. *The Journal of Positive Psychology*, *10*(1), 3–6. https://doi.org/10.1080/17439760.2014.888582

Seligman, M., Steen, T., Park, N., & Peterson, C. (2005). Positive psychology progress: Empirical validation of interventions. *The American Psychologist*, *60*(5), 410–421. https://doi.org/10.1037/0003-066X.60.5.410

Seppälä, E. (2014, September 15). 18 science-backed reasons to try loving-kindness meditation. *Psychology Today*. https://www.psychologytoday.com/ca/blog/feeling-it/201409/18-science-backed-reasons-try-loving-kindness-meditation

Sheldon, K., Frederickson, B., Rathunde, K., & Csikszentmihalyi, M. (2000). *Positive psychology manifesto: Akumal 2 meeting.* https://ppc.sas.upenn.edu/sites/default/files/Positive Psychology Manifesto.docx

Sheldon, Kennon M., & Lyubomirsky, S. (2019). Revisiting the sustainable happiness model and pie chart: Can happiness be successfully pursued? *The Journal of Positive Psychology, 16*(2), 145–154. https://doi.org/10.1080/17439760.2019.1689421

Shetty, J. (2020). *Think like a monk: Train your mind for peace and purpose every day.* Simon & Schuster.

Simmons, J. P., & Simonsohn, U. (2017). Power posing: P-curving the evidence. *Psychological Science, 28*(5), 687–693. https://doi.org/10.1177/0956797616658563

Simons, D. (2010, March 10). *Selective attention test.* YouTube. https://www.youtube.com/watch?v=vJG698U2Mvo

Statistics Canada. (2017). *Families, households and marital status: Key results from the 2016 Census.* https://www150.statcan.gc.ca/n1/daily-quotidien/170802/dq170802a-eng.htm

Strack, F., Martin, L., & Stepper, S. (1988). Inhibiting and facilitating conditions of the human smile: A nonobtrusive test of the facial feedback hypothesis. *Journal of Personality and Social Psychology, 54*(5), 768–777. https://doi.org/10.1037/0022-3514.54.5.768

Steger, M. (2010). *The meaning in life questionnaire (MLO).* Michael F. Steger: Laboratory for the study of meaning and quality of life. http://www.michaelfsteger.com/wp-content/uploads/2013/12/MLQ-description-scoring-and-feedback-packet.pdf

Steger, M. (2012). Experiencing meaning in life: Optimal functioning at the nexus of well-being, psychopathology, and spirituality. In P. Wong (Ed.), *The human quest for meaning: Theories, research, and applications* (2nd ed., pp. 165–184). Routledge.

Strecher, V. (2016). *Life on purpose: How living for what matters most changes everything.* HarperOne.

Tedeschi, R., & Calhoun, L. (2004). Posttraumatic growth: Conceptual foundations and empirical evidence. *Psychological Inquiry, 15*(1), 1-18. https://www.researchgate.net/publication/247504165_Tedeschi_RG_Calhoun_LGPosttraumatic_growth_conceptual_foundations_and_empirical_evidence_Psychol_Inq_151_1-18

Treleaven, D. (2018). *Trauma-sensitive mindfulness: Practices for safe healing.* WW Norton.

Tuleja, E. (2022). *Intercultural communication for global business: How leaders communicate for success* (2nd ed.). Routledge.

Twenge, J. (2020, January 22). Six facts about screens and teen mental health that a recent New York Times' article ignores. *Institute for Family Studies.* https://ifstudies.org/blog/six-facts-about-screens-and-teen-mental-health-that a-recent-new-york-times-article-ignores

Twenge, J., & Martin, G. (2020). Gender differences in associations between digital media use and psychological well-being: Evidence from three large datasets. *Journal of Adolescence, 79*(1), 91–102. https://doi.org/10.1016/j.adolescence.2019.12.018

Uhls, Y., Michikyan, M., Morris, J., Garcia, D., Small, G., Zgourou, E., & Greenfield, P. (2014). Five days at outdoor education camp without screens improves preteen skills with nonverbal emotion cues. *Computers in Human Behavior, 39*, 387–392. https://doi.org/10.1016/j.chb.2014.05.036

University of Texas at Austin. (2020, May 19). Cooperation can be contagious particularly when people see the benefit for others. *ScienceDaily.* https://www.sciencedaily.com/releases/2020/05/200519144452.htm

VIA Institute on Character. (n.d.). *Character strengths.* https://www.viacharacter.org/character-strengths-via

Waldinger, R. (2015, November). *What makes a good life? Lessons from the longest study on happiness* [Video]. TED. https://www.ted.com/talks/robert_waldinger_what_makes_a_good_life_lessons_from_the_longest_study_on_happiness/transcript?language=en

Waldinger, R., & Schulz, M. (2023). *The good life: Lessons from the world's longest scientific study of happiness.* Simon & Schuster

Walker, M. (2017). *Why we sleep: Unlocking the power of sleep and dreams.* Simon & Schuster.

Walker, M. (2019, April). *Sleep is your superpower* [Video]. TED. https://www.ted.com/talks/matt_walker_sleep_is_your_superpower?language=en

Walker, M. (2020a). *Hacking your memory – with sleep* [Video]. TED. https://www.ted.com/talks/matt_walker_hacking_your_memory_with_sleep

Walker, M. (2020b). *How sleep affects your emotions* [Video]. TED. https://www.ted.com/talks/matt_walker_how_sleep_affects_your_emotions?language=en

Walker, M. (2020c). *6 tips for better sleep* [Video]. TED. https://www.ted.com/talks/matt_walker_6_tips_for_better_sleep?referrer=playlist-sleeping_with_science

Ward, A., Duke, K., Gneezy, A., & Bos, M. (2017). Brain drain: The mere presence of one's own smartphone reduces available cognitive capacity. *Journal of the Association for Consumer Research, 2*(2), 140–154. https://doi.org/10.1086/691462

Ware, B. (2019). *Top five regrets of the dying: A life transformed by the dearly departing.* Hay House.

Weir, K. (2013). More than job satisfaction. *Monitor on Psychology, 44*, 39–42. https://www.apa.org/monitor/2013/12/job-satisfaction

Weir, K. (2020). Nurtured by nature. *Monitor on Psychology, 51*(3). https://www.apa.org/monitor/2020/04/nurtured-nature

Whillans, A. (2020). *Time smart: How to reclaim your time and live a happier life.* Harvard Business Publishing.

Willen, S., Williamson, A., Walsh, C., Hyman, M., & Tootle, W. (2021). Rethinking flourishing: Critical insights and qualitative perspectives from the U.S. Midwest. *SSM — Mental Health, 2*, 1–13. https://doi.org/10.1016/j.ssmmh.2021.100057

Williams, L., & Bargh, J. (2008). Experiencing physical warmth promotes interpersonal warmth. *Science, 322*, 606–607. https://doi.org/10.1126/science.1162548

Wrzesniewski, A., & Dutton, J. (2001). Crafting a job: Revisioning employees as active crafters of their work. *Academy of Management Review, 26*(2), 179–201. https://positiveorgs.bus.umich.edu/wp-content/uploads/Crafting-a-Job_Revisioning-Employees.pdf

Yang, L. (2021, January 31). In the moments of non-awakening. *Lion's Roar.* https://www.lionsroar.com/in-the-moments-of-non-awakening/

Young, S. (2011). *Five ways to know yourself: An introduction to basic mindfulness.* Unified Mindfulness. https://unifiedmindfulness.com/wp-content/uploads/2016/02/Five-Ways-to-Know-Yourself.pdf

Young, S. (2016). *What is mindfulness?* Shinzen Young. https://www.shinzen.org/wp-content/uploads/2016/08/WhatIsMindfulness_SY_Public_ver1.5.pdf